Joseph Raffael:
The California Years, 1969-1978

Organized by Thomas H. Garver for the
San Francisco Museum of Modern Art
January 20 - March 5, 1978

This exhibition and catalog have been
generously supported by grants from
Security Pacific Bank and the National
Endowment for the Arts, Washington, D.C.,
a Federal agency.

San Francisco Museum of Modern Art
January 20 - March 5, 1978

Des Moines Art Center, Iowa
March 27 - April 30, 1978

Joslyn Art Museum, Omaha, Nebraska
July 7 - August 20, 1978

Newport Harbor Art Museum,
Newport Beach, California
September 15 - November 26, 1978

The Denver Art Museum, Colorado
January 20 - March 4, 1979

Table of Contents

Library of Congress Cataloging in Publication Data
Main entry under title:

Joseph Raffael: the California years, 1969-1978.

Includes a catalog of the exhibition, which was also held at other museums, Mar. 27, 1978-Mar. 4, 1979.

Bibliography: p.

1. Raffael, Joseph, 1933-   —Exhibitions.
I. Raffael, Joseph, 1933-   II. Garver, Thomas H.
III. San Francisco Museum of Modern Art.

N6537.R23A4   1978   759.13   77-28193

Lenders to the Exhibition

American Telephone and Telegraph, New York
Stan Berde, San Francisco
Jack E. Chachkes, New York
Chase Manhattan Bank, New York
Jim Copening, Lagunitas, California
First National Bank, Council Bluffs, Iowa
Walter C. Goodman, San Francisco
Mr. and Mrs. Walter J. Haas,
Lagunitas, California
Mr. and Mrs. Wellington S. Henderson,
Hillsborough, California
Hirshhorn Museum and Sculpture Garden,
Smithsonian Institution, Washington, D.C.
Mr. and Mrs. Bruce W. Hyman, San Francisco
Mr. and Mrs. William C. Janss,
Sun Valley, Idaho
Joslyn Art Museum, Omaha, Nebraska
Stephen Kaltenbach, Woodland, California
Mr. and Mrs. Leon Kogut, Evanston, Illinois
Long Beach Museum of Art, California
Byron Meyer, San Francisco
Nancy Hoffman Gallery, New York
The Oakland Museum, California
William S. Picher, San Francisco
Joseph Raffael, San Geronimo, California
Roy Boyd Gallery, Chicago
Security Pacific Bank
Shaklee Corporation, Emeryville, California
A. James Speyer, Chicago
Robert Stormont, Woodland, California
University Art Museum, Berkeley, California
Willard and Susan Webb, New York
Whitney Museum of American Art, New York

Foreword

The Joseph Raffael exhibition represents one of those rare museum projects which can be declared to have been a pleasure from its inception to its culmination. The initial proposal for the exhibition was put forward by Thomas H. Garver, then Curator of Exhibitions at The Fine Arts Museums of San Francisco and now Director of the Newport Harbor Art Museum in Southern California. Due to scheduling problems it was not possible to place the Raffael exhibition in the program of The Fine Arts Museums so, by mutual agreement, Mr. Garver was appointed to be guest curator of the show for the San Francisco Museum of Modern Art.

Mutual respect between the artist and the curator eased the often difficult process of work selection and established a solid basis for the development of Mr. Garver's primary essay. Robert Hughes, art critic for *Time* magazine, who has followed Mr. Raffael's creative development from its beginnings in New York, agreed to write an additional essay for the catalog.

It has also been our very good fortune to have responsive colleagues at the institutions to which this exhibition will be circulated: James T. Demetrion at the Des Moines Art Center; Ruth H. Cloudman at the Joslyn Art Museum; Thomas Maythem and Lewis Story at The Denver Art Museum; and Thomas Garver at the Newport Harbor Art Museum.

While an important single event on our schedule, this exhibition also represents one more in a series of major one-artist exhibitions designed to document many of

America's best artists who have chosen to live and to work in the San Francisco Bay Area.

Not only this Museum but The Oakland Museum and the University Art Museum, Berkeley, have presented in-depth exhibitions, documented by solid catalogs. Perhaps by the mid-1990's, Bay Area museums may catch up with the area's creators. At the very least, art libraries across the country will have developed a respectable shelf of documentation from this region.

Security Pacific Bank has been exceptionally generous in providing major funding for the development of the entire project, and the National Endowment for the Arts, a Federal agency in Washington, D.C., has provided an important grant in support of the exhibition.

Mr. Raffael's dealers, Nancy Hoffman in New York, Roy Boyd in Chicago and John Berggruen in San Francisco, have been helpful in many ways. In addition, Walter C. Goodman, William S. Picher and Byron Meyer, all of San Francisco, have generously supported the catalog production. Special thanks are due as well to Mrs. Walter A. Haas, Jr., and Mrs. James Crane for their work on behalf of the exhibition.

Joseph Raffael has been especially helpful and cooperative throughout the organization of this project. He has generously provided us with records and photographs to make this catalog more complete and his thoughtful time in responding to our many questions and needs has been invaluable.

Many hours of Museum staff time have brought about the exhibition's realization. Michael McCone, Deputy Director, has

overseen many of the administrative particulars which inevitably are involved in such a major undertaking. Karen Tsujimoto, Assistant Curator, has coordinated all of the details with the guest curator and the artist in obtaining loans and preparing the catalog; she has been ably assisted by Louise Katzman, Curatorial Assistant, Katherine Church Holland, Research Associate, and Dorothy Martinson, Curatorial Secretary. Susan King, Registrar, and her assistant, Nona Ghent, handled the many transportation details, and Julius Wasserstein and his staff have effected the installation of the exhibition.

To those mentioned above and especially to the lenders to the exhibition, my real thanks.

Henry T. Hopkins
Director

Acknowledgments

This catalog was written at Joseph and Judy Raffael's house in Marin County. It was quiet at the time I wrote it, Joseph was in the Far East, Judy in the Midwest with the younger children, and Robert and Matthew, their teen-age sons, rose late, flashed about for a bit, and then vanished until the next morning. The location gave me the opportunity to write this introduction at a difficult moment in my life, the transit between positions from curator at The Fine Arts Museums of San Francisco to Director of the Newport Harbor Art Museum in Newport Beach, California.

I am grateful to Joseph and Judy for having made their place available. I am also grateful to Natasha Nicholson, my wife, for her willingness to take on most of the struggle and anxiety of packing in order to give me the time to prepare this catalog.

Joseph and Judy Raffael's warmth and friendship with me over the years have far exceeded the ritualized cooperation between an artist and one who may make an exhibition of his art. I am pleased to have been a part of their family for a moment. They and their children, Robert, Matthew, Rachel and Reuben, have all been of help to me by answering questions, but more importantly, by showing me by example how a family works supportively to the benefit of all of its members.

Judy Raffael, who is herself a remarkable artist in a wide range of media, has not only discussed Joseph's work with clarity and feeling but has also articulated in the most passionate terms the importance she sees in their development together, and the independent strength they have derived from their shared relationship.

Many of the ideas expressed here have come from two long interviews taped with Joseph in December of 1976 and another with Judy in March of 1977. Quotes in the introduction from the interviews, not acknowledged in footnotes, have come from these sources.

Joseph's assistants, Korda D. Cordes and Eric Chu, have been most helpful in assembling photographs, articles and other materials I have needed. Karen Tsujimoto, Assistant Curator of the San Francisco Museum of Modern Art, has not only been competent, she has been diligent, efficient and above all humorous.

To the lenders, whose names are acknowledged elsewhere, I must give warmest thanks for their willingness to part with paintings they love (and owners of Joseph Raffael's works feel very strongly about them) for a year's period. Special thanks go to Nancy Hoffman in New York, the artist's dealer, who tempers her professional relationship with a long-term understanding and warm personal friendship shared with Joseph and his family. She and the artist's two other dealers, John Berggruen in San Francisco and Roy Boyd in Chicago, have helped underwrite the cost of this catalog, as have Wally Goodman, Stan Picher and Byron Meyer of San Francisco.

My thanks also go to Marty Meade, Lagunitas, California and Julie Helfrich, Newport Beach, California, for typing this manuscript.

T.H.G.
San Geronimo/Newport Beach, California

Statement by the Artist

There are many, many people who have meant a great deal to me both personally and professionally. It would be an impossibility for me to list each and every one of them here.

However, at this point in my life, I particularly appreciate those who early on in my professional life offered me encouragement and support. I would like to choose one to represent the many. It was the writer Bill Wilson, of New York City, who first wrote an article about me and my work. It was written in the mid-60's, and its understanding and compassion moves me to this day.

I also wish to thank Nancy Hoffman, who has been more than a dealer for me, she has been a true friend.

I want to thank Karen Tsujimoto and the staff of the San Francisco Museum of Modern Art for the extraordinary attention and care they have given this show.

I also want to thank Bob Hughes, whose mind and independent spirit has been a meaningful source of nourishment, encouragement, and pleasure for me over the years.

And finally, my thanks to Tom Garver, who had the idea for this exhibition in the first place. He has followed through, from the beginning, with openness, flexibility, and thoroughness. His sensitivity as friend and curator touches me deeply.

This acknowledgment would not be complete without my thanking Judy Raffael. These paintings would not be as they are if I had not known Judy.

Joseph Raffael
October 10, 1977
San Geronimo, California

A Sunday morning in October. Joseph Raffael is in his studio working on Ch'i, perhaps one-third completed. It is hung on the wall by a block and tackle system that allows the painting to be dropped into a slot in the floor when the artist is working on the top or hoisted to the ceiling when he is painting the bottom. He is seated in an old oak side chair to paint the lower center portion. A large, homemade taboret is at his right side, and a small brass floor lamp, rather precariously taped to a short stepladder, stands to his left, lighting a small area of the canvas. It is the only artificial illumination in the studio. Raffael takes a moment to clean the palette, a sheet of plate glass, and to arrange the photograph from which he is working, an 11 × 14 inch color print taped to a cardboard backing which is in turn taped to the canvas. The photo, with a small trapezoidal area corresponding to the area which he is painting marked with tape, is fixed to the canvas about 8 to 10 inches above the area to be painted. Raffael reviews the palette colors, indigo, rose doré, Indian yellow, manganese blue, burnt umber, burnt sienna, rose madder pale, sap green. Black is almost never used. The canvas has been primed with seven coats of gesso, and that is the only white used in the painting.

The title of the painting, Ch'i (cat. no. 23), is indicative of the way Raffael now thinks of his work and selects the images he will paint. The genesis image for the painting was a photo Raffael had made a few months previously of a small fragment of a pond and shore, an anonymous bit of landscape made all the more so by the way the land growth toppled into the water, the weeds, grasses and twigs gradually disappearing into the rippled, cloudy water. Thus the transition from one medium, from one "element" to another, is indeterminate, a nature rich in reference but obscure in its answers. Ch'i the title Raffael has chosen—before the painting is complete—is a Chinese word, the concept of which was first introduced to him in the writing of Alan Watts. Ch'i is the vital force in nature, a dynamic breath of life which cannot be measured or really described in words, but which "surrounds man as water surrounds a fish."

A few weeks earlier, before beginning the painting, Raffael had projected the transparency from which the work is taken onto the canvas and drawn outlines around the color shapes with a hard pencil. The lines are very pale, almost invisible from a distance of a few feet, and eliminate the need to grid the canvas.

Raffael begins to paint. Seated in his chair, his feet on the floor, knees almost touching the canvas, he selects a small round brush. He offers a caveat. "Each painting is painted differently," he says. Sometimes he works with a large brush, sometimes a small one, and since painting Landscape several years ago, his painting method changes from day to day. On this painting he uses a small, soft brush because of the myriad shimmering areas to be constructed, and today he holds the brush like a wand, grasping it at least eight inches from the end. Quickly mixing pigment and turpentine diluent, he traces the penciled outlines in color. Some are filled in with the outline color or with another color variant or left white as highlights. A flicker of yellow on the canvas, a floating leaf sinking below the water's surface, is grayed off with the thinnest wash of blue. "A lesson I learned from Albers, you don't need to use black to make gray." He continues, using the tip of the brush for a line or twisting it across an area for a wider stroke, knowing that one side of the brush may have more pigment than the other, and a quick twist will vary the intensity of the wash. "The brush does the work."

He sits within inches of the painting, looking only at several square inches of canvas. Head still, eyes moving up to the photo and down to the painting, the right hand mixing colors, washing the brush, painting in an almost disembodied way. The connection between hand and brush seems so frail. He studiously ignores the growing finished areas of the painting, concentrating only on those few square inches in front of him until the work will be completed. The period of actual creation is a time of physical intensity, preceded and followed perhaps by more contemplative or concerned states of mind when he may consider the quality of the work as a whole, or contemplate the next work to be made. But now those considerations are held in abeyance.

There is an interruption, a dispute with Matthew, his 16 year old son, about the correct way to pull poison oak which grows around the studio; it flares into a full-scale argument. Both leave in anger. The empty studio allows a moment to examine the painting and its genesis photograph together. The differences are profound. Raffael not only expands the size of the image, but expands the repertoire of organic forms and much amplifies the color and contrast range as well. The photo contains only the barest suggestions of the pinks, madders, subtle clear blues, and transparent russets which form so much of the painting. Nor does the photo possess the rich umber shadows shot through the dazzling highlights, each surrounded by thin lines of neutral colors: gray-green, faded blue, taupe, which buffer the light, shadow and colors against one another. This linear skein, frequently so subtle as to be more implied than seen, is necessary to support the color. It is, in a sense, the intellection, the subdued yet important thought structure, that both defines and controls the color exuberance.

Raffael returns. The argument has ended in a way not untypical of the household. Matthew has stated his position with force, clarity and passion, and his father acknowledges its correctness; the air is cleared, the anger is dissipated. Matthew receives a day free from chores. The poison oak remains to grow another day.

Dear Tom,

These words from Wallace Stevens' "The Man With The Blue Guitar" have filled me with their meaning since my days at Yale. I wanted you to read them. They've been really helpful to me & my work.

XXXII

Throw away the lights, the definitions,
And say of what you see in the dark

That it is this or that it is that,
But do not use the rotted names.

How should you walk in that space and know
Nothing of the madness of space,

Nothing of its jocular procreations?
Throw the lights away, Nothing must stand

Between you and the shapes you take
When the crust of shape has been destroyed

You as you are? You are yourself.
The blue guitar surprises you.

Joseph Raffael was born Joseph Raffaele in Brooklyn, New York, on February 22, 1933, the only son and third child of Joseph Marino Raffaele and Cora Kaelin Raffaele. His father was Sicilian, born in Australia where he lived very briefly before his parents again emigrated, this time to the United States. His mother was a combination of an Irish mother and Swiss-German father who had a large potato farm on Long Island.

Raffael was a frail child physically, but one with an active mind. The early part of his life, spent largely alone, was a time of deep feeling, which fortunately worked to set his sensibilities in the right direction. It was a time, he reflects, as being neither unpleasant nor particularly happy, yet the right prologue for the life to come.

Raffael's father was a remote and silent man, "introverted and unrealized," handsome in a style that Raffael recalls as resembling George Raft. He managed an A & P grocery store in Brooklyn for almost forty years, but his work week was broken up and he was almost never at home. The socialization of his son was also remote. He never showed the younger Raffael how to be with people.[1] His mother was just the opposite, "a rosy extrovert," and much more influential on her young son. In fact, he was practically raised by his mother, his two sisters and several female relatives who encouraged him by example to develop his feeling and intuitive sensibilities.

Very early in life Raffael developed a curious way of perceiving his surroundings. As a young child he spoke very little; in fact, he now thinks he was communicating by other means, or certainly receiving information in ways other than the linear, spoken word. He "gazed" instead of talked, receiving and utilizing information visually and directly, not verbally. Unfocusing his eyes, he would (and still does) gaze at objects, dissolving them into essences of form, light and color. The gaze engendered a state of reverie, which he describes as a "slippery place, expressed fully only through poetics," more metaphor and suggestion than fantasy, in which specific three-dimensional relationships were changed into generalized lateral pattern-puzzles across the field of view.

The only picture in his house was a Maxfield Parrish reproduction which hung over the living room radiator. A small image of enormous scale and intense color, it portrayed two wraith-like young women gazing into a foreground pool with giant urns on either side, framing a long vista across a great sun-streaked valley. Perhaps more important to Raffael than the Maxfield Parrish was the wallpaper of the Brooklyn house. He vividly recalls gazing in a dream state at its interweaving patterns, regarding it now as his first experience with "art." The Maxfield Parrish, the wallpaper, the patterned rugs and a pair of porcelain vases with floral designs on the mantelpiece, were the stuff of fantasy to him, and he would spend hours looking at them, or lying by the radiator copying illustrations from magazines while listening to the radio.

During his childhood years his parents summered on the tip of Long Island near Orient Point. One year their house was on the water and at high tide the waves would practically lap the back porch. He liked the country and enjoyed the water, swimming or just gazing at it when a summer ear infection kept him on the shore. Raffael describes these summers as helping to let him enter the phenomena of nature, but as a witness, not a participant.

High school was a revelation because for the first time he came in contact with people of similar interests. He studied at The Brooklyn Museum Art School on weekends, working with Isaac Soyer, one of the three painting Soyer brothers, drawing the nude in class and after class drawing sculpture in the Museum's collection. Following class he would walk to the public library a few blocks away to look at art books and check out classical records.

He also loved the movies with a passion and would go to New York on weekends, or to theatres in Brooklyn on the weekdays, to see three or four films a week. He particularly enjoyed the big musicals of the forties and he now sees the need for these films as "intuitive nourishment" which answered his unconscious desires for large size and transparency of color-image, the qualities he also enjoyed in his wallpaper.

After graduation from high school, Raffael entered Cooper Union School of Art and Architecture in Manhattan. It was an experience that not only focused his energies to new levels of attention and commitment but, most importantly, expanded his sensibilities as to the nature of art as well. His artistic ambitions began to form at this time and he knew he wanted to live his life as an artist. While at Cooper Union he became better connected to art as a universal and metaphorical endeavor through one of his instructors, an artist named Sidney Delevante, who encouraged Raffael to think of himself as a poet, connected to an identity beyond a specific image, to a higher, more extended state of being. Delevante verbalized and reinforced what Raffael had been doing intuitively in his gazing. Two other instructors at Cooper Union also strongly affected him: John Ferren for his coloristic ideas and Leo Manso for his lyrical approach to abstraction.

After Cooper Union he won a fellowship to Yale-Norfolk summer school and then, through the help of Bernard Chaet, entered

Yale University to complete work for his B.F.A. degree. Much has been made of Raffael's studying with the master of color, Josef Albers. The relationship between the aging master and his pupil was not easy, but the experience was crucial to Raffael for the understanding of the light and life to be found in color. Further, Albers encouraged him to be his own man and to resist pressures towards stylistic conformity which were very strong at that time.

He much admired Abstract Expressionist paintings, but his favorite artists in that vein were artists of a more coloristic, lyrical and "constructed" persuasion, including Willem de Kooning, Philip Guston, Bradley Walker Tomlin and Arshile Gorky. While he was nurtured as an Abstract Expressionist, Raffael never thought of himself as such. He was an abstract painter working primarily from photographs of natural phenomena. Perhaps the most important non-art experience of his Yale years was the discovery of poetry, an art of metaphor in another medium, and he felt particularly close to the poems of Wallace Stevens.

Following his graduation in 1956, Raffael moved back to New York and began work as a free lance fabric designer in a textile studio. It was a profitable experience for his art. He improved the facility and speed of his drawing, as well as improving its expressive character. He also learned more about color and visual structure and how to repeat designs in various media. It was good technical training and proved to be useful in the future. He also continued to paint during this period, working at night, and in 1958 received a Fulbright scholarship to study and paint in Florence. He spent about a year

and a half there, living in a guest house on the grounds of a handsome Tuscan villa overlooking the city. He worked hard painting, making watercolors and producing a calligraphed book. It was his first trip to Europe and he was highly moved by the powerful paintings of the old masters, artists who had been motivated by a spirituality which Raffael had neither perceived nor understood previously. The Italian landscape, too, nature consciously ordered but not defiled, extended a strong generative influence on his work, which was so closely connected to nature as a root source.

In early 1960 he returned to the United States and continued textile design for a time, but he stopped when he finally began selling his own work privately in sufficient quantity that he could modestly support himself. Raffael at this time received support from Maurice Tuchman, then a curator at the Guggenheim Museum, and in 1962 he went to Italy, unaware that the trip was to be the genesis of the first great change cycle of his adult life. He painted first in Spoleto, then was a guest at a villa near Florence where he painted landscapes until the fall of the year, when he returned to New York to continue working on his first one-person exhibition in New York at the d'Arcy Gallery, scheduled for February of 1963.

In February of that year he became critically ill with hepatitis, presumed to have been contacted when he was in Italy. Raffael was in the hospital nine weeks, coming out just in time to see the last day of his exhibition. He also saw Robert Rauschenberg's monumental survey exhibition at the Jewish Museum before going to Puerto Rico to recuperate.

His paintings prior to his illness had been of informal hard-edged shapes, highly colored forms outlined with edges or lines of darker or contrasting color. The color shapes were sometimes opaque or brushed in with thin

translucent washes. The sources continued to be natural images from published sources, although virtually totally obscured in their transliteration from printed page to canvas.

After his return to New York he was allowed to paint only a few hours a day and his work underwent a substantial change. "Little by little white paint began covering color—paint and color—covered in white." The shift in his work was seen by Raffael as a paradigm of his past, and an indication that his past was being relentlessly obliterated by the present, with his illness marking a passage into another sphere to which he was beginning to respond.

Events moved swiftly. The assassination of John Kennedy and the national paroxysm of anguish that followed subdued and influenced but did not slow the revolutions which were changing art in New York. There was a "joy" about new art then which was almost universally felt there. Exhibitions of works by Jasper Johns and the Green Gallery shows of George Segal and Claes Oldenburg, among others, were particularly influential on art at the time.

Reality and illusion increasingly obtruded in Raffael's paintings, and since his illness he had become highly sensitized to his own mortality and vulnerability. "A few years ago I was in the hospital; I almost died. When I got out, I could only work, do anything, for about three hours a day. Time became important to me, and life, in a very sensual way; I began observing things. Moving my fingers became an event. I was stunned by life and living things."[2]

By late 1963 his painting had become representational, a dense overlayed collage of images painted from newspapers and magazines, most of them involving physical prowess and endurance, fragments of runners, swimmers or boxers layered against other more atmospheric images, a sunset over the ocean, a redwood grove, or

references to individuals and objects marked by topical vulnerability or power. Jackie Kennedy in widow's weeds, Bobby Kennedy, and Fidel Castro were among them, along with wrecked cars or a surgeon's hands suturing an incision. All these were rendered with crisp illustrative precision in oil wash on a white ground. Gradually, however, the images thinned and their relationships to one another became simpler.

In May of 1964, he began work on a cycle of white ground paintings generally credited as his first mature work. These paintings, simple in structure, were highly complex in their allusions. Raffael's life, Kennedy's death, Rauschenberg's composition, the spirit and energy in New York which encouraged work in a figurative manner: all formed part of the psychological structure of his paintings at this time. Raffael worked from boxes of clippings which he took from magazines and other sources. He would select an image, paint it without preliminary drawing in a thin wash, working with a curvilinear stroke directly on a heavily gessoed canvas. Upon completion of that image, he would either juxtapose another image to the first, or paint those second and subsequent images on other canvases, which would then be assembled together as one painting.

The construction of the paintings was closely related to collage, and in fact he produced a large number of collages in the late sixties and early seventies although he almost never used the collaged image in his paintings. Collage and painting were two separate, if closely parallel, media.

The white ground paintings were seemingly uninflected, the images randomly selected. Morto Padre, 1966 (illustrated, not in exhibition), is an example. At the time Raffael

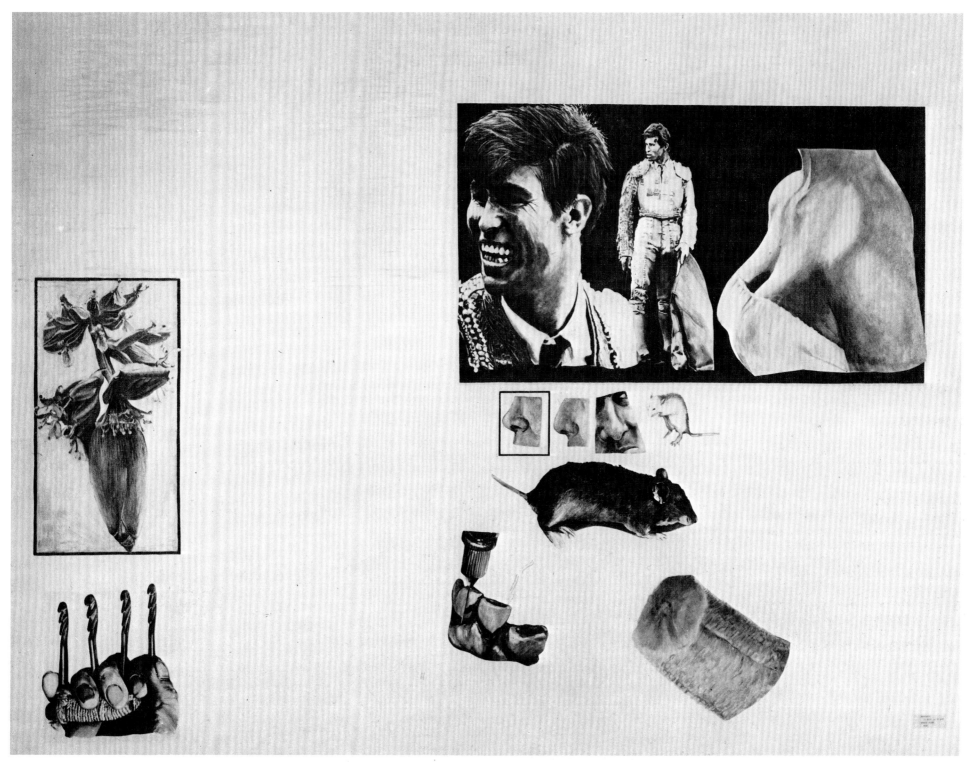

Morto Padre, 1966, oil on canvas, 60×80″
Collection of the artist
(not in exhibition)

acknowledged only that he was painting a factual juxtaposition of objects; what the viewer saw in these works was resonant with that individual to those intuitions in themselves. Yet, in *Morto Padre*, a memorial to his father and an Italian friend's father who had both recently died, the images are psychically loaded and equate physical desirability—a disembodied bosom, a matador, with vulnerability and pain—the dentist's needle piercing tender gums, the mice to be experimented upon, a piece of banana, a metaphor perhaps for a truncated phallus. The message, at least at this point some years later, seems clear; no pleasure may be undertaken without risk. To open oneself to outside experience is daring the onset of pain. To live is to die.

These works have an edgy, almost angry, physicality about them, and Raffael now acknowledges that they were much more personal and associative than he admitted at the time they were executed, that they were, in fact, "a daily descriptive record of *angst*." The images were highly personal to him, even though he could not discuss their interpretation or autobiographical character until years later.

In 1965 Raffael began showing at the Stable Gallery and in the fall of 1966, the night of the opening of his second exhibition there, he flew to California to begin a short teaching assignment at the University of California at Davis, a position which had been offered to him suddenly. Before his departure he had thought of California as being "like Miami Beach, drinks at poolside under swaying palms." He was pleasantly surprised at what he found.

The 1966 trip was the opening wedge of a cycle of change that far exceeded the influence of his illness of several years

before. Raffael took a small apartment on Nob Hill in San Francisco and commuted to Sacramento, ninety miles east, twice a week. It was there that he met several other artists, including William Allan and William Wiley, in what must have been a most remarkable department. Raffael became particularly friendly with Allan and Wiley, with whom he has developed strong and lasting friendships.

He responded wholeheartedly to the California of the sixties and was intrigued and fascinated by the "broadness" and expansivity of the life and art of his California colleagues. Some of the artists could incorporate families, many other activities and a multiplicity of media, films, painting and sculpture, into their life styles. In New York he had not permitted himself many personal interests outside of his profession, but Raffael was now ready to expand his own life experiences.

He returned to New York in early 1967, excited by his discoveries. The white ground paintings continued, albeit with differences. Elements of collage and assemblage began finding their way into the work, previously so pristinely painted, as an influence of some of the artists in Northern California who used material of this nature; Raffael, however, used it in an orderly and constructed way. The year 1967 was spent consolidating the person, and the artist's production diminished as he began to involve himself in the slow restructuring of his life. As one aspect of this restructuring, he visited an astrologer, who after researching his name, discovered that numerologically it matched Jack Kennedy's. She urged him to change his name slightly to Joseph Raffael, and he did so at once, despite the shock expressed by his dealer and friends.

In early 1967 he began a wordless correspondence, a communication of long-distance collage, with Judy Davis, a

young woman from California who had moved with her two young boys to Bennington, Vermont, to teach theatre costume and set design at Bennington College. The correspondence, part of Ray Johnson's "Correspondence School," had been started by Raffael at Bill Wiley's suggestion and was enthusiastically returned by Judy Davis.

In the last month of that year, the white ground paintings came to an end. He had begun transcendental meditation and was working to extend the new wholeness he felt as an individual into his art. Despite his references to the contrary, the white ground paintings were psychological constructs, visual rebus puzzles of intellectual and emotional fragmentation, which he was eager to eliminate through a reformation of his painting style and imagistic sources. He now concentrated on large single forms and the first unitary images, drawn again from magazine illustrations, were two objects from Tutankhamen's tomb, the great gold mask and the head of a cheetah worked in gold with a tear of lapis lazuli or Egyptian paste. In these images and others to follow, including a jewel encrusted crown and Beethoven's death mask as modeled by Rodin, Raffael set the direction for his work of the next ten years.

Tut, 1968 (illustrated, not in exhibition), and *Cheetah*, 1968, were both cut from *Paris Match* illustrations and both had the distortions of color one finds in high-speed printing. Raffael liked them because these image sources were not simply flat replications of three-dimensional objects but individual variations of them. At this point he enjoyed working from reproductions several times removed from reality because they

Tut, 1968, oil on canvas, 77½ × 59″
Collection Stephen Booke
(not in exhibition)

15

Crown, 1969, oil on canvas, 77½×60″
Collection The Wichita Art Museum, Kansas
(not in exhibition)

were not reality and allowed him, in fact, to take his own license with these forms. Much more importantly, however, he consciously began to seek images of objects which had heroic or noble qualities, which possessed "a higher glow to them." In the white ground paintings the images had been anonymous and topical, powerful for the moment perhaps, but not historically lasting. Now he sought identification with an imagery of a long past artist or artisan which contained a rich historical identity along with the light and specular glow, the luxuriousness which Raffael loved and which he painted with such seeming ease.

He continued to transfer the unitary images directly onto the canvas without grid or projection, drawing the outlines of the form directly in paint, then immediately filling in the outline, a technique that he uses to this day. This process created curious compositional anachronisms. In *Crown*, 1969 (illustrated, not in exhibition), the crown image itself is curiously distorted with the top and left edge of the form strangely cropped. Yet this seeming awkwardness is a saving grace, for it mitigates a too easy interpretation of the image as an icon of light and glittering luxury, a triumph of the artist's facility. The painting is as much an individual object as the thing it portrays.

Although the acceptance of representational art was growing rapidly, many New York critics still regarded figurative painters as ". . . marginal courtiers or saboteurs around the thrones of Abstract artists."[3] If the climate for representational art was warming, there still existed strong pressures for conformity, particularly in the definition of a recognizable, crystalline individual style, one of the lingering remnants perhaps of the biographical aspects of Abstract Expressionism which equated individual

painterly form with the identity of the individual. Raffael's desire for wholeness required images that extended their meaning beyond formal concerns, and more than ever it was imperative that he avoid a schism between what he felt and what he painted. He was facile enough to paint anything, but the energy in his works had to extend beyond replication rendered in a stylistically recognizable way. His philosophy was already beginning to diverge from other New York New Realists, to whom stylistic "hand" and intellectual remove were paramount. Richard Estes, perhaps New York's current premier representational painter, summed up that attitude a few years later. "I don't enjoy looking at the things I paint, so why should you enjoy it? I enjoy painting it because of all the things I can do with it. I am not trying to make propaganda for New York. . . I think I would tear down most of the places I paint."[4]

By mid-1968 Raffael's concern that his work as an artist not become separate from his identity as a man was becoming intense, and he was beginning to consider leaving New York to seek a situation that would allow him more psychic space. A fortuitous event encouraged that change. During the course of the year Raffael's wordless correspondence with Judy Davis had been increasing. In July of 1968 they met in New York and the day after left for Bennington. They were married in September and in an instant he became husband and twice a father. Bennington, while a way-station, was a vital transition point. His marriage gave him an identity beyond "artist" and Vermont offered, for the first time in his adult life, a sense of place beyond the studio.

Judy Raffael had been much involved with Native American history and imagery at the time, and Raffael, looking through her books, found powerful visual source material for his own work. He started the first of the Indian paintings in Vermont, a series

which was to become an informal group of perhaps eight such ethnic images of which *Blackfoot*, 1970 (cat. no. 1), and *Pomo*, 1970 (cat. no. 2), are included in this exhibition.

Raffael's use of photographs—silver print, transparency or half-tone—as image sources has come under such wide discussion that it might be well to comment on it in these two works. Clearly the photos from which the Indian paintings derived were historical and not in color, but Raffael's modernist sensibilities, obvious in his transmutation of the images in the paintings to many times life-size, cannot be said to be the same aesthetic that motivates the seamless replications of Richard Estes or the mechanical detachment of Chuck Close. Raffael has, in fact, taken the widest latitude with his original source materials. Little flicks and twists of color swirl across the drawn structure; a web of lines serves, particularly in *Pomo*, to emphasize the anatomical features of the face. Like van Gogh (whom Raffael has long admired for the passion and feeling he brought to his life and work), Raffael used this web in *Pomo* to shape the forehead as it fans out above the bridge of the nose and to structure the high cheekbones and the corners of the mouth. Light, too, aids the structure in the intense highlights of the exposed white ground of the canvas. Color, which Raffael handles with such skill, is used in profusion, but with such tonal restraint as to suggest monochrome. Yet the effect of monochrome is infused with subtle energy articulated by the color, an effect which would be impossible to achieve in true monochrome.

Too, these images of weather-beaten faces are no longer directly appealing as in the gold or jewels of his works of a short while

earlier. There is an intensity and disquietude about these paintings that mark Raffael's commited attachment to his original image sources. Imagery is not simply the baggage necessary to achieve a specific formal appearance, but is the vehicle through which the artist works to achieve transcendental responses which each perceptor must extend beyond the visible data supplied. Photography and other flat imagistic sources serve Raffael no more or no less than the modern day replacement for sketches in the field or preparatory color studies. He can and does shift color and other formal elements between the source and completed work with impunity.

By early 1969 Raffael was interested in returning to California because it was a place where he could be alone in his development but not isolated from contact with art ideas or his artist friends. He was offered jobs at the University of California, Berkeley, and Sacramento State College, and they moved west in the summer of 1969. Shortly after their arrival, the family moved to a house in San Geronimo Valley in Marin County, about thirty miles north of San Francisco. The house was ideal for them and has been a strong influence on his work because its location emphasizes both a sense of nature and also of place. Located halfway up the southern slope of the San Geronimo Valley, it is set in a grove of second growth redwoods. Its placement offers several vistas, each very different. From the back of the house the trees rise cathedral-like, while to the front the vista opens to the northern shoulder of the valley, more open, with meadows, pale green or

golden, depending on the season, studded with blue-green live oaks and small groves of young redwoods. Overhead, several skylights set into the roof show the trees fanning out above. Built as a summer house many years ago, the building's outlines have been changed and softened by several additions. A small studio was constructed near the house, followed several years later by a larger studio, which provides work space for both Raffaels.

Their third child, Rachel, was born in 1969, followed in 1972 by Reuben, their fourth. Judy Raffael has continued to expand her own aesthetic vision and for the last few years has been drawing and working in watercolor. She and Joseph Raffael have extended strong influence on one another in both life and art. The benefits of this relationship are beyond the scope of this short introduction, yet both agree that the quality, intensity and quantity of work they have produced has been greatly enhanced by their relationship.

Before Reuben's Birth, 1971,
collage on board, 19⅞ × 15¼"
Courtesy John Berggruen Gallery,
San Francisco (not in exhibition)

The Paintings from California

In 1970 Joseph Raffael painted a large work of a young duck beginning its flight to freedom. This painting, *Release*, 1970 (cat. no. 3), shows to the left the fingers of the hand that held the duck. They have opened and the bird, almost filling the width of the nine foot canvas, beats its wings violently as it takes to the air. The painting is one of his first images dealing with natural phenomena, plants, animals and landscape, and it is also autobiographical, Raffael's visual recognition of a new beginning he was experiencing.

In the eight years that have intervened, Raffael's work has undergone as profound a change in point of view as that which energized the white ground paintings. The change, however, has been manifested less in a stylistic sense than in the man himself and in the purposes he now sees his art as serving. He found that "California did not so much alter his style as to allow him to work less self-consciously within it."[5] During the course of those years, Raffael has worked on half a dozen informally structured sets of images, although within the last two years the structure of the sets has diminished to the point where one can describe the most recent works only as being involved with nature close-up, and water is often present.

Raffael had already started work on the series of massive portrait heads when he arrived in California. Shortly before coming West he also experimented with the use of shaped canvases, the only work which used collage as a source, and, after his arrival, with assemblages of found objects in relief and in the round. Yet inexorably Raffael was drawn to natural phenomena with an intensity that had not previously attracted his interest. In 1971 he produced a suite of animal portraits that were the high water-mark of an image cycle that began with *Tut*.

They include *Lion*, 1971 (cat. no. 4), *Lizard*, 1971 (cat. no. 5), and *Seal*, 1971 (cat. no. 6), included in this exhibition. They are iconic in their centrality and rigidly balanced composition and are the closest Raffael came to fulfilling the dictates of New York New Realist technical maxims, which have been described as ". . . large scale canvases, magnified, close-up viewpoints, frontalized imagery, thematic serializations, cropped composition, non-hieratic arrangement of forms, clarity of visual focus, utilization of a photograph, display of technical virtuosity, and an awareness of a field-like flatness of the painting's surface."[6] It would seem that the energy of New York lingered on in these rather overpowering images which combine the luxuriousness and voluptuousness of surface, light and repetitive flickering strokes of thin oil paint upon the brilliant white ground. They may well have been painted in anticipation of what the New York art world would have expected of him. While the paintings that were to follow the animals make use of New Realist elements in measure, they shift away from a subject matter of such specificity and clarity of composition to a view of nature which seeks to become more universal by becoming less specific in its painted illusionism.

In early 1972 he returned to New York for the opening of an exhibition of his recent paintings. He had not been back in three years and found that his sense of direct communication with that art world, so highly developed when he had lived there, had become disrupted. Issues which motivated his work and those motivating New York were no longer congruent. He returned to California and to the birth of his son Reuben with a sense of re-affirmation of his own position and a strong desire to paint a work which would document it.

He began his biggest painting to date, probably the most important single work of his career, *Landscape* (illustrated, not in

exhibition), and it is a major shadow on this exhibition that it cannot be seen here. Taken from an illustration in a European magazine of an Argentinian glacier seen through an opening in dense and startling tropical foliage in the foreground, it is almost eight feet high and eleven feet long. The canvas virtually filled the end of his small studio, and Raffael never saw it from a distance greater than fifteen feet until it was finished and moved outside. He used a soft and rather floppy brush to begin the painting, working first on the big leaves along the top and left side of the canvas. They were painted so openly that Raffael was profoundly concerned that he was losing his technique. He pressed on and discovered that for some inexplicable reason he was changing his painting style for each part of the work; the rocks, glacier, sky and water were all painted differently. It was a painful and confusing time for him. He didn't and still doesn't know why this discontinuity occurred at this time or why it began with *Landscape*. Yet this discontinuous technique is now a touchstone of all his subsequent work, and while almost invisible in the overall effect of any one painting, it is essential to it, for these shifts articulate the surface with bursts of power and cycles of quiescence, areas of expansion and compression which move laterally across the canvas plane, energizing the painted surface, which in most recent work has become increasingly flat and abstracted.

In concept and execution, the painting of *Landscape* was regarded as a cleansing ritual, requiring as much physical and psychological endurance as to tax even Raffael's polished technique. Its painting took seven months and changed the course of his art, as it was the manifest indication of

Landscape, 1972, oil on canvas, 92×132″
Collection Robert Mayer Estate
(not in exhibition)

a change in himself. "I have been trying to kill the critic in me—in my art, and by the time I reached the point of painting *Landscape*, I had lost the power of criticism."[7] For Raffael, criticism as he uses it is a "linear second self—beyond the artist, judging good and bad, major and minor." He laid to rest at last the earlier alter ego he had battled for so long. He was surprised and pleased with the variety of responses the painting generated, which indicated to him both the painting's universal resonance with individuals who saw it and the artist's oneness with the viewers. "It's one of the few paintings that I've seen which becomes the reflection of the viewer's mind rather than the reflection of the artist's mind . . . I was the viewer, too, and as I was painting I was amazed that the painting was coming out of the brush. I just loved it. It was like having a wonderful conversation with someone or meeting someone . . . That's the way it was, continual discovery."[8]

Susan Ehrlich has written tellingly about *Landscape* as evidence of Raffael's strong commitment to Jungian principles of archetype and synchronicity, using as well-taken evidence the choice of his subject matter, which ranges across non-urban and non-Western cultures, both ancient and modern, including plants and animals. She sees this as evidence of ". . . the sense of connection that he feels with all mankind regardless of temporal or geographic distances . . . as well as his feelings concerning the psychic continuity of all living things."[9] She also postulates that Raffael's compulsion to paint *Landscape* and his stated amazement as to how the painting took form are further evidence of Jung's definition of the artist as being an individual who is keenly susceptible and responsive to compelling forces of the

collective unconscious in producing his work. Raffael is well aware of Jung's concepts and accepts them as part of the artist's function in the transcendental experience.

Landscape is the first of Raffael's paintings to achieve a reality which truly transcends its original sources. His pleasure in finding that the painting reflected the viewer's mind rather than the artist's is evidence of his desire to find ways of creating works of art which act on some level as universal constants or equivalents. Raffael went on to state his belief about this painting that the artist has—humbly—been placed in a divinely directed position. "Artists are servants of God in the sense that they have insights into the universal. They live from a mysterious place. Artists work from a void and go outward from that point . . . Their will has nothing to do with it, and that's why making art is in a sense very religious."[10] Raffael, in his own way, seems to be reiterating the words of an artist he admires, Robert Rauschenberg, who said, "Painting relates to both art and life. Neither can be made. (I try to act in that gap between the two.)" Both men, so different in style and point of view, yet fully conscious of their own identities, acknowledge forces from without which mysteriously aid in the shaping of their sensibilities as artists.

While working on *Landscape*, Raffael was visited by the painter Bill Allan, a devoted fisherman who had made a number of transparencies of the rivers on which he fished, with the thought they would make excellent paintings and that Raffael could really paint the wetness of water. Raffael accepted the slides, although the thought of working so directly from another artist friend's images bothered him at first. The photographs were good, however, and fitted into his emerging vision to paint a nature that was general, drawing universal themes

from specific images which were themselves unidentifiable and non-hieratic. He wanted to make pure paintings which he defined as illusionistic but free of definite images, and water was substance and abstraction at the same moment. Water changed its character with its location and offered the artist the challenge to paint transparency through reflection, color and light within a colorless fluid.

The first five of the water paintings, of which *Water Painting II*, 1973 (cat. no. 9), is included in this exhibition, were executed from Bill Allan's slides in a burst of energy beginning in late 1972. Critics and writers have searched for historical parallels to these paintings. Monet is a name frequently cited as a touchstone for the imagery, while others have suggested other Impressionists, French and American, and even Jackson Pollock. While Raffael's paintings exhibit an "allover" surface, Pollock's aims and methodologies are too remote from Raffael to be seriously considered, although both are men who have been much influenced by nature. Monet broke the hegemony of the single vanishing point perspective in his late works but was less involved in light than paint structure, and Monet's water is more about paint application than Raffael's, which is about light and liquid translucency, liquid applied as a liquid.

In the water paintings and more directly in the scenes of water lilies which followed, Raffael was on a balance point. His works, while painted in an allover manner (closer, however, to Mark Tobey, Milton Resnick, or even Agnes Martin than Pollock), were not abstract, nor were they replicatory illusionism of the sort practiced by other New

Realist artists. Nor, too, were Raffael's paintings the application of optical or scientific principles of paint handling as practiced by Seurat, nor the rigorous imposition of an intellectual order upon banal reality found in Chuck Close. On occasion Raffael's paintings, or even portions of them, might tilt off the balance toward one or the other of these areas, but it is to his credit that his work cannot be easily locked into equivalent verbal descriptive systems.

In 1973, following an exhibition of the first five water paintings in New York, the Raffaels took a vacation in the Scottish highlands. It was a trip of rejuvenation and Raffael, who had now begun to make his own photographs, eagerly documented the lakes and rivers of the area. He had not intended to continue the water paintings past the original group of about ten, but the incredible vitality of the Scottish experience changed that. Immediately upon returning, he resigned from his teaching position to devote all his time to painting and began to work on an expanded group of water paintings, which included *Black Craig Shore*, 1974 (cat. no. 12), and *Highland Magic*, 1975 (cat. no. 14).

In the late spring of 1974, Raffael, while working at a very high level of energy, undertook another project requiring not only physical stamina but emotional and intellectual vulnerability as well. It was a project which grew from his curiosity and desire to experiment with technique. During the previous year or so, he had been working extensively with watercolor as a parallel medium to oils and enjoyed the fluidity and luminosity he could achieve with great speed. Further, about the time the water paintings began, Rachel, his daughter,

then two years old, would come to the studio and Raffael would give her sheets of typewriter paper and watercolors so she could paint too. She would dash off her paintings with such verve and pleasure that he envied her ingenuous innocence and wished that he could capture in his art her sense of delight, spontaneity and directness.

In May of that year, Raffael abandoned illusionism entirely, painting a large cycle of watercolors and about a half a dozen large canvases in a space of less than two months. Splattered, washed, and dripped, the large oils were never seen and, with one exception, were all destroyed by the artist. Photographs show the works to be bursts of energy without attachment to subject matter. They are a reprise of Abstract Expressionism, yet much freer than any work Raffael had painted in the fifties and early sixties when he was most influenced by that movement. One may postulate that like *Landscape*, these paintings were a voyage into the unknown, an area of explosive freedom in the sense of action painting, much beyond what the artist had ever done and, in fact, wished to continue to do. They were abstract, gestural, physical painting, in which issues of illusion and space were operant only in the abstract sense. Enjoyable to create, these paintings were not invested with the ambiguity of nature—suggested and transcendent— found in his figurative paintings. As a result, they were not rich with the communication of both specific and abstract issues on many levels which Raffael so eagerly sought. Only one painting of this period survived, *4th of July*, 1974 (cat. no. 13). It combined much of this free form energy, yet, by the artist's choice, was more structural and less emotional than the others, although it did not identify itself as a painting of nature. It is interesting to compare it to *Muir Creek I*,

1973 (cat. no. 8), which it slightly resembles in tonality, to study the differences between a painting in which structure retains the core of illusion and one in which illusion is no longer present. *4th of July*, if less central to Raffael's total *oeuvre*, is important, for it and the cycle of nonrepresentational paintings that preceded it served to define for him the parameters within which he could operate most comfortably and most effectively. This cycle of paintings freed his hand to paint in any manner he chose, from tight to loose, from meticulous detail to freely running washes.

Raffael expanded the outer bounds of feelings in *Landscape* and similarly exploited the outer limits of his technical interests in the cycle culminating with *4th of July*. His work of the next two years took a curious bifurcate course, moving in cycles between what might be characterized as a high form of natural illusionism, in which the identification of nature was co-equal with painterly form, and another more structural mode, where the artist's calligraphic stroke dominated the subject. One senses in the paintings of 1975 and 1976 a movement between the man as a feeling propagandist for a transcendent nature, where the "one" was the symbol for "all," and his wish to express himself as an artist, an individual man with an identifiable style.

The watercolors, such as *14 Fish*, 1977 (cat. no. 36), a recent work, and a number of smaller oils not included in this exhibition, reflect the latter structural sensibility in the looser stroke, the more open calligraphy and play of forms across the surface plane, issues that have preoccupied modernist artists for years. Yet on occasion at this time, major works also reflected these more personal abstract sensibilities. *Black Craig Shore*, 1974 (cat. no. 12) and *Kona*, 1975

12
Detail (approx. actual size),
Black Craig Shore, 1974

(cat. no. 16), are two examples of the predominance of the structural mode. *Black Craig Shore* is a painting of light, almost removed from representational imagery, a painting which floats across the imagistic/non-representational line. It is a painting about painting, with drips and runs crossing its surface, mitigating illusion. Raffael in his discussions of this painting quoted a stanza from Wallace Stevens. "Poetry is the subject of the poem/From this the poem issues . . ."[11]

Highland Magic, 1975 (cat. no. 14), and *Lily Painting; Hilo II*, 1975 (cat. no. 17), are examples of the artist working with nature on a more directly illusionistic level. The photograph from which *Highland Magic* is taken, however, and the completed work bear little resemblance to one another. Like the photo for *Ch'i* (cat. no. 23), the image for *Highland Magic* has been much expanded in color and emotion as well. Raffael has not simply changed the photograph to a painting but has charged the work with a coruscant energy, investing the work with more color information than was present in the original source. The "implications" of water, its transparency and reflection, its response to color and light, are all magnificently exploited and its identity as water thereby intensified. In the photograph one sees slightly turbid water at the shore in a moment of photographic stop-time, but water in the painting more closely approaches the platonic ideal as one of the four natural elements of the classical world. *Lily Painting; Hilo II* is closer to the original transparency and is perhaps the high point to date of his preoccupation with light as a

potent natural force that illuminates, reflects, transmits and finally obliterates detail in its own intensity.

In early 1976 Raffael received a commission to completely fill an architectural space covering the end wall of a large living room. The painting, *Black Spring*, 1976 (cat. no. 20), is his largest work to date but was executed with much less doubt than *Landscape*, and within the work the issues of image and structure begin to fuse together. Its size and relatively severe composition may have aided in melding them, for one is less conscious here of struggle of structure and illusion than of an interlocking visual system in which issues of the general or the specific—in focus/out of focus—are carried along together, co-equally and unconsciously. It is a painting that opens itself to the spectator without need for intellection yet can easily withstand rigorous intellectual review. It is as rich in multifaceted information as in its visual execution.

This synthesis was finally completed in late 1976 in *A Frog in Its Pond*, 1976 (cat. no. 19), and the paintings subsequent to it, including *Wild Iris*, 1977 (cat. no. 24), *Blue Pond*, *Winter Shore*, 1977 (cat. no. 22), and *Ch'i*, 1977 (cat. no. 23), in this exhibition. Consider the similarities in all four paintings. Unlike many of their predecessors, none of these paintings bespeak either uncommon technical facility nor monumental natural effect, although they all possess both. All are quieter, drawn from photographs which in themselves are unprepossessing. To say that Raffael "copied" them would be a misunderstanding of the word. Judy Raffael, commenting on her husband's use of photography, has said, "Joseph uses the structure of the photograph as a guide to his feelings." They are important records of a moment that impresses itself upon the artist,

an interlock between humanity and nature which she has described as the "visual identification of a state of mind." Each of these four works is a field painting, tied to modernist sensibilities by the overall non-centricity of composition and a noninflective execution as well as flatness of image. Further, there is emphasis on a transmogrification of image character by vastly increasing its size, particularly marked in *A Frog in Its Pond* and *Wild Iris*. Earlier paintings are thunderous in their subject matter, icons of illusionism, and aggressive in their technical bravura, in comparison to the meditative tranquility realized in these late works, which are more austere images, non-focused, and assert themselves in a less doctrinaire way. Their emotional spread and the depth of what one can only describe as the effects on one's "spirit" or "soul" or "feelings" is correspondingly more profound and more broadly based. One responds more slowly to them. They are quiet music, not a martial air, but their quiet power lasts much longer.

Each is a *tabula semi-rasa*, a feeling state extended through a kind of illusionism, a slate-not-quite-clean, but rich rather with information quietly and subtly offered, which extends itself to the viewer in an almost religious way. These paintings are, as Jan Butterfield has so aptly observed, "Paintings for those who are not afraid of beauty."[12] Raffael has said that his work is "all autobiographical, on an illusory level." And if so, these paintings would indicate that he is approaching that "still quiet center of the soul" which permits calm reflection within an active mind. He has also said that he wants to communicate, to affect many people and to affect them broadly and profoundly by poetry. He seeks to make an art that "looks at you rather than have you look at it," that will open the ego centered perception of spectators in a way in which they will enter with the painting into a mutual exploration of feeling in a non-linear, non-intellectual way.

The works of Joseph Raffael have undergone profound change, a change of concept and breadth of emotional intensity, rather than of discreet formal structure. This change has been paralleled by the artist's own development, a transformation pre-figured by William Wilson in 1966. At that time Wilson acutely sensed Raffael's future direction when he said, "This respect for things as in the Franciscan mood that credits every creature with sensation, personality, and mind is a version of self-respect because the things are embodiments of feeling, objectifications of emotion: they are parts of a self that is thinking and feeling with the things of this world. These are paintings that care about things; they show that an absence of feelings anywhere in the world is a cause of concern to the self."[13]

Thomas H. Garver

Notes

[1] Raffael is very conscious of his familial past and is determined not to repeat it. He is very close to his children, and the dynamics of the household, while sometimes stormy, are very open, loving and supportive. His children are in turn free to lead their own lives in an independent way, yet tempered by the responsibilities they recognize they owe to the family unit.

[2] "Paint, Flesh, Vesuvius," an interview with G.R. Swenson, *Arts Magazine*, November 1966.

[3] Lawrence Alloway, "Art as Likeness," *Arts Magazine*, May 1967.

[4] Richard Estes, in an interview with Linda Chase and Ted McBurnett, "The Photo Realists: Twelve Interviews," *Art in America*, November-December 1972.

[5] Robert Hughes, *Time*, October 15, 1973.

[6] Susan Ehrlich, "Joseph Raffael, *Lily Painting; Hilo II*," an unpublished paper prepared for the Department of Fine Arts, California State University, Northridge, 1976.

[7] "In Art with Joseph Raffael," an interview with Lynne Zickerman, *Daily Californian Arts Magazine*, October 20, 1972.

[8] *Ibid.*

[9] Susan Ehrlich, *op. cit.*

[10] Lynne Zickerman, *op. cit.*

[11] Wallace Stevens, *Man with a Blue Guitar*, stanza XXII.

Poetry is the subject of the poem,
From this the poem issues and

To this returns. Between the two,
Between issue and return, there is

An absence of reality,
Things as they are. Or so we say.

But are these separate? Is it
An absence for the poem, which acquires

Its true appearance there, sun's green,
Cloud's red, earth feeling, sky that thinks?

From these it takes. Perhaps it gives,
In the universal intercourse.

[12] Jan Butterfield, " 'I Have Always Copied': an Interview with Joseph Raffael," *Arts Magazine*, October 1976.

[13] William Wilson, "The Paintings of Joe Raffaele: In the Franciscan Mood," *Art and Artists*, September 1966.

Below: Original 35-mm slide taken by the artist

Top right: Color print made from 35-mm slide

Bottom right: Detail from painting, *A Frog in Its Pond*, 1977

A Note on Joseph Raffael

None of us has an innocent eye, and the bird which (so the story in Pliny goes) demonstrated its own naivety by flying down to peck at a bunch of painted grapes by the Greek artist Zeuxis is extinct. The problem is not that we are incapable of being fooled (nobody is) but that the social conditions of illusion, thanks to photography, have changed; they scarcely include painting any more. It seems almost unimaginable that five hundred years ago people stood as trapped by the two-dimensional fiction of an altarpiece as visitors to Disneyworld, today, are convinced by the illusion of laser holography. Yet the greatest service photography gave to the art of painting was to subliminally teach everyone the truth of Magritte's phrase, "This is not a pipe." (Of course it isn't; it is a painting.) Under these conditions of reduced illusion, the mind begins to enjoy the limits of realism.

Obviously, not everything in the world can be painted. There is a certain level of scrutiny below which pigment, an oily paste smeared on a surface with a frayed stick, cannot go. Jan van Eyck's account of the pores on Chancellor Rollin's nose, or the reflection of a room in the highlight on a glass, may seem infinite in its detail—and is meant to, since he apparently wanted painting to function as a metaphor of God's eye, keeping everything in the world in existence by knowing about it—but it is still limited by the size of the smallest brush he could make. In Velázquez, the relationship between the infrastructure of painting, the clots and streaks and scribbles left by the brush, and the way they mix on the eyeball to provoke illusion, becomes a declared subject of art; and that relationship, ever since, has been the primary issue of realist painting. It is the thing that photography, despite its limitless capacity for appropriating the world, cannot successfully

replicate—the area in which its mechanical and automatic nature becomes apparent. Grain is not handwriting.

Both the look and the scale of Raffael's photo-derived images have a lot to do with this fact. To begin with, the water paintings are not verifiable. There is no reality against which they can be checked in detail, form by form, the way one can run a reality-test on conventional photo-realist images by putting them alongside a real Burger King stand or a Honda 750. The subject vanished long before the painting began. "It has nothing of its own," wrote Leonardo, who spent more years in the obsessive scrutiny of water than any artist in history, "but takes everything, changing into as many different natures as there are different places on its course, acting just like the mirror, which takes in as many images as there are things passing in front of it." The only possible *aide-memoire* for an artist who wants to paint water in turbulent motion is the photograph. (Raffael's work has many merits, but Leonardo's precision of memory, power of notation and almost preternatural quickness of eye are not, one need scarcely add, among them; and in any case the bubbles and vortices of Leonardo's own water studies are full of stylistic generalizations.) Nevertheless, the 35-mm slide has its inherent limits. Project it on a canvas eight feet wide and look at it from a range of a few feet, the distance between a painter and his work: the detail fogs out into a mass of indeterminate patches which are, literally, emulsified, being made of emulsion. What Raffael does with this no-man's-land of color is the clue to the ordering of his work. He is still, at root, an artist deeply imbued with the kind of allover painting, the knitted and skeined flatness of surface, that surrounded him as a student in New York 20 years ago. Every blur and patch in the blown-up slide must therefore be made active, brought into articulate shape, by the linear scribbling of a fine wet brush. This has little to do with copying. Nor is it "rendering" in the stolid

photo-realist sense of the term. It is more like the reordering of an image from the inside out, bones and all. One is left with an extraordinary delicacy of surface: blooms of flight, fragile ziggurats of bubbles—Raffael's favorite repeated shape is an egg—and slow drifts of sparkling, aqueous color. The transparency of the paint gives one the impression that water is describing itself. It is a vulnerable system of painting, this build-up of atmospheric micro-forms within a vague whole; and there are passages in Raffael's work which fail through the jewelled, fetishistic accumulation of detail which turns substance into a kind of visionary frog-spawn. But they are infrequent. As a rule Raffael shows the infallible mark of a "natural" painter, truth of tone. To make one vibrant passage is not a big thing; but to fill a large canvas with light and air so that every rock, leaf and water splash holds its just ration of space through a prolonged, inch-by-inch inspection—that is the real test.

As Tom Garver points out in his catalog essay for this show, Raffael is deeply interested in the Taoist idea of *ch'i*: not as a conventional bit of Marin County chinoiserie, but as a goal of work. "If the spirit of the painter is not keen and broad at the same time," remarked a Ming writer, Li Ji-Hua, "he cannot succeed and make his point. That which is called spirit-resonance (*ch'i yun*) is inborn in the man . . . he may fill up his picture with fine details and develop skill and strength in every direction, but what interest have such things for superior people?" *Ch'i* was understood to be a cosmic property, the Chinese equivalent to the Greek *pneuma* or the Hindu *prana*: a spiritual force imparting life to substance. In painting, *ch'i* meant something more than "vitality," but that was its rough sense: a spontaneous rightness of mark and meaning.

Ink painting was considered the supreme vehicle for the manifestation of *ch'i*,

because of its extreme delicacy and responsiveness; the life of a form hung on the subtlest unconscious pressure of a brush-point. Raffael does not work in monochrome; nor does his method of painting, calligraphic but patiently built up, confront him with the same taxing obligation to get the stroke right, first time for last. He can correct, and incessantly does so. Nevertheless his passion for subjects which lie just on this side of indeterminancy—the ambiguous shallows of water, or the shape of a lily pad half-dissolved in a flux of light—makes clear his desire to keep the thinnest membrane between instinct and description, and so to "Let the *ch'i* in." In his best moments, Raffael ceases to be a realist artist; the technical apparatus of photography and enlargement drops away, the studio practice fades into the background, the biography of his development as an artist ceases to obtrude (although it does matter), and we are left with a very American figure recognizable from his 19th-century prototypes along the Hudson River and the Yosemite Valley, the painter as Italian altar boy in the cathedral of nature. " 'What,' it will be Question'd, 'When the Sun rises, do you not see a round disk of fire somewhat like a Guinea?' O no, no, I see an Innumerable company of the Heavenly host crying 'Holy, Holy, Holy is the Lord God Almighty.' I question not my Corporeal or Vegetative Eye any more than I would Question a Window concerning a Sight. I look through it and not with it." Blake's famous note describes the sublime extremity of that state of mind to whose lower ground Joseph Raffael's paintings belong. In a pulpy and faddist culture, glazed with its promises of instant uplift, here is a visionary artist; and as visionaries do, he returns the world to us in its lost freshness.

Robert Hughes

23
Ch'i, 1977

1
Blackfoot, 1970

2
Pomo, 1970

20
Black Spring, 1976

3
Release, 1970

4
Lion, 1971

5
Lizard, 1971

6
Seal, 1971

7
Loon, 1972

8
Muir Creek I, 1973

9
Water Painting II, 1973

10
Water Painting V, 1973

11
Water Painting VI, 1973

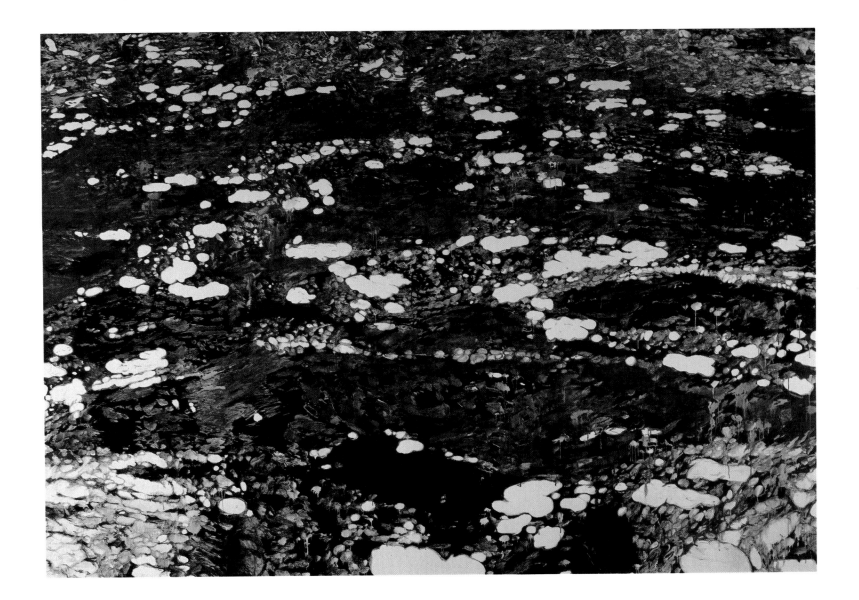

12
Black Craig Shore, 1974

13
4th of July, 1974

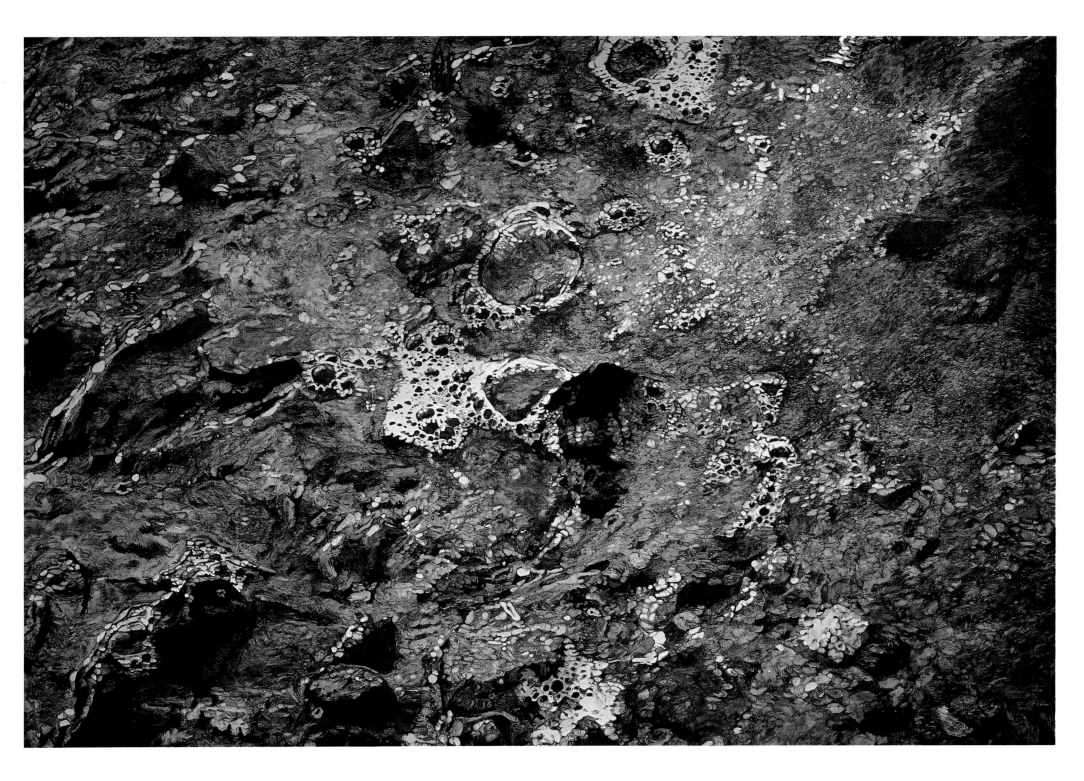

14
Highland Magic, 1975

15
Hilo, 1975

16
Kona, 1975

17
Lily Painting; Hilo II, 1975

18
Mystic Lily, 1975

19
A Frog in Its Pond, 1976

21
likeadream, 1976

22
Blue Pond, Winter Shore, 1977

24
Wild Iris, 1977

26
Untitled, 1973

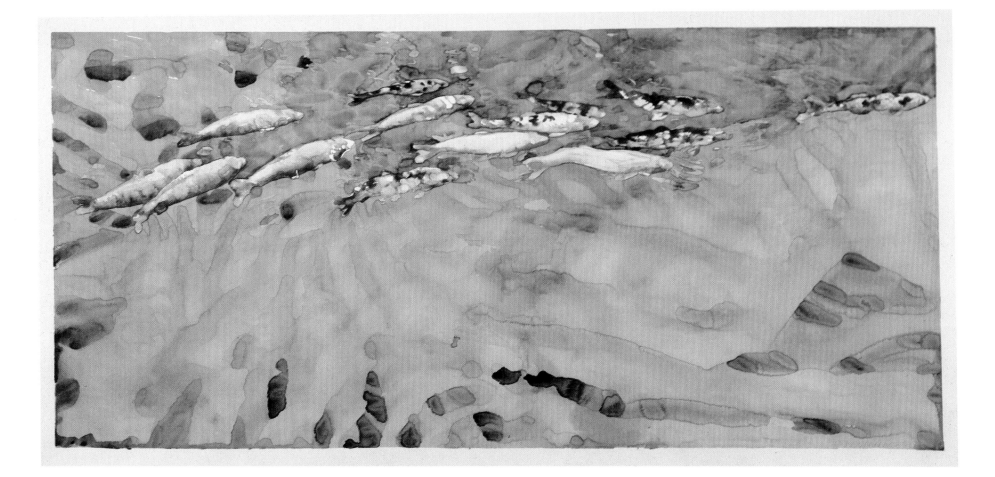

36
14 Fish, 1977

Checklist of the Exhibition

In the listing of dimensions, height precedes width.

Paintings

1 *Blackfoot*, 1970, oil on canvas, 79½×61½" (201.9×156.2 cm.) Collection Joslyn Art Museum, Omaha, Nebraska

2 *Pomo*, 1970, oil on canvas, 79×59½" (200.7×151.1 cm.) Collection University Art Museum, Berkeley, California, Purchased with the aid of funds from the National Endowment for the Arts

3 *Release*, 1970, oil on canvas, 75×108" (190.5×274.3 cm.) Collection First National Bank, Council Bluffs, Iowa

4 *Lion*, 1971, oil on canvas, 84×84" (213.4×213.4 cm.) Collection of the artist

5 *Lizard*, 1971, oil on canvas, 84×84" (213.4×213.4 cm.) Collection of the artist

6 *Seal*, 1971, oil on canvas, 85½×85½" (217.2×217.2 cm.) Collection Long Beach Museum of Art, California

7 *Loon*, 1972, oil on canvas, 48×48" (121.9×121.9 cm.) Collection Stephen Kaltenbach, Woodland, California

8 *Muir Creek I*, 1973, oil on canvas, 66×81" (167.6×205.6 cm.) Collection Willard and Susan Webb, New York

9 *Water Painting II*, 1973, oil on canvas, 78×114" (198.1×289.6 cm.) Collection Security Pacific Bank (For exhibition in San Francisco only)

10 *Water Painting V*, 1973, oil on canvas, 78×114¼" (198.1×290.2 cm.) Collection Whitney Museum of American Art, New York

11 *Water Painting VI*, 1973, oil on canvas, 78×114" (198.1×289.6 cm.) Collection Jack E. Chachkes, New York

12 *Black Craig Shore*, 1974, oil on canvas, 78×114" (198.1×289.6 cm.) Collection Mr. and Mrs. William C. Janss, Sun Valley, Idaho

13 *4th of July*, 1974, oil on canvas, 78×84" (198.1×213.4 cm.) Collection of the artist

14 *Highland Magic*, 1975, oil on canvas, 96×114" (243.8×289.6 cm.) Private Collection, New York

15 *Hilo*, 1975, oil on canvas, 90×66" (228.6×167.6 cm.) Collection Byron Meyer, San Francisco

16 *Kona*, 1975, oil on canvas, 90×66" (228.6×167.6 cm.) Collection Robert Stormont, Woodland, California

17 *Lily Painting; Hilo II*, 1975, oil on canvas, 84×132" (213.4×335.3 cm.) Collection The Oakland Museum, California, Gift of the Collectors Gallery and the National Endowment for the Arts (For exhibition in San Francisco only)

18 *Mystic Lily*, 1975, oil on canvas, 60×60" (152.4×152.4 cm.) Collection Mr. and Mrs. Wellington S. Henderson, Hillsborough, California

19 *A Frog in Its Pond*, 1976, oil on canvas, 78×114" (198.1×289.6 cm.) Private Collection, Chicago

20 *Black Spring*, 1976, oil on canvas, triptych: 82×220" overall (208.3×558.8 cm.) Collection Walter C. Goodman and William S. Picher, San Francisco

21 *likeadream*, 1976, oil on canvas, 66×90" (167.6×228.6 cm.) Courtesy Nancy Hoffman Gallery, New York

22 *Blue Pond, Winter Shore*, 1977, oil on canvas, 78×114" (198.1×289.6 cm.) Collection of the artist

23 *Ch'i*, 1977, oil on canvas, 96×144" (243.8×365.8 cm.) Collection Nancy Hoffman Gallery, New York

24 *Wild Iris*, 1977, oil on canvas, 78×114" (198.1×289.6 cm.) Collection Shaklee Corporation, Emeryville, California (For exhibition in San Francisco and Des Moines only)

Watercolors and Drawings

25 *Pelican*, 1972, watercolor on paper, 22×14" (55.9×35.6 cm.) Collection A. James Speyer, Chicago

26 *Untitled*, 1973, watercolor on paper, 30×45" (76.2×114.3 cm.) Collection of the artist

27 *Duck with Reflection*, 1975, watercolor on paper, 21½×31" (54.6×78.7 cm.) Collection of the artist

28 *Rock*, 1975, ink on paper, 22½×30" (57.2×76.2 cm.) Collection of the artist

29 *Haiku Birds*, 1976, watercolor on paper, 25×38½" (63.5×97.8 cm.) Courtesy Nancy Hoffman Gallery, New York

30 *Lily*, 1976, watercolor on paper, 29½×46" (74.9×116.8 cm.) Collection Jim Copening, Lagunitas, California

31 *Mallard*, 1976, charcoal on paper, 21¾×35" (55.2×88.9 cm.) Collection Walter C. Goodman and William S. Picher, San Francisco

32 *Season of the Frog*, 1976, watercolor on paper, 25½×35¼" (64.8×89.5 cm.) Collection of the artist

33 *3 Birds*, 1976, watercolor on paper, 28⅝×39¾" (72.7×101.0 cm.) Collection Mr. and Mrs. Leon Kogut, Evanston, Illinois

34 *Wisteria*, 1976, watercolor on paper, 40×28¾" (101.6×73.0 cm.) Courtesy Roy Boyd Gallery, Chicago

35 *Fish Dream*, 1977, watercolor and pastel on paper, 35×45" (88.9×114.3 cm.) Courtesy Nancy Hoffman Gallery, New York

36 *14 Fish*, 1977, watercolor on paper, 43¼×89¾" (109.9×228.0 cm.) Collection Stan Berde, San Francisco

37 *Luma Lily*, 1977, watercolor on paper, 35×45" (88.9×114.3 cm.) Collection Mr. and Mrs. Walter J. Haas, Lagunitas, California (For exhibition in San Francisco only)

38 *Lundy Valley Lily*, 1977, watercolor on paper, 45×92" (114.3×233.7 cm.) Collection American Telephone and Telegraph, New York

39 *Spring Branch*, 1977, watercolor on paper, 35×45" (88.9×114.3 cm.) Collection Mr. and Mrs. Bruce W. Hyman, San Francisco (For exhibition in San Francisco only)

40 *2 Goldfish*, 1977, watercolor on paper, 35×45″ (88.9×114.3 cm.) Collection Chase Manhattan Bank, New York

41 *Zwanck Night*, 1977, watercolor on paper, 33⅞×44¼″ (86.1×112.4 cm.) Collection Hirshhorn Museum and Sculpture Garden, Smithsonian Institution, Washington, D.C.

Prints

42 *The Sea, Wind, and Stars Series: I*, 1974, series of five monoprints (color lithographic process), each 20¾×30″ (52.7×76.2 cm.) Courtesy Nancy Hoffman Gallery, New York

43 *The Sea, Wind, and Stars Series: II*, 1974, series of six monoprints (color lithographic process), each 20¾×30″ (52.7×76.2 cm.) Courtesy Nancy Hoffman Gallery, New York

44 *Moonlight*, 1975, color aquatint, 42/75, 23×31″ (58.4×78.7 cm.) Courtesy of the artist

45 *White Lily*, 1976, color aquatint, 25/50, 42×30″ (106.7×76.2 cm.) Courtesy of the artist

46 *Black and White Lily*, 1977, lithograph, 2/20, 22×28″ (55.9×71.1 cm.) Courtesy of the artist

47 *11 Fish*, 1978, color lithograph, 2/40, 28×22″ (71.1×55.9 cm.) Courtesy of the artist

1933
Born, February 22, Brooklyn, New York.

1951-54
Attended Cooper Union School of Art and Architecture, New York. Studied with Sidney Delevante and Leo Manso.

1954
Received fellowship, Yale University-Norfolk School of Music and Art, Norfolk, Connecticut (summer).

1954-56
Attended Yale University School of Art, New Haven, Connecticut, B.F.A., 1956. While at Yale, studied with Josef Albers and James Brooks. Moved to New York City after graduation from Yale; worked in textile studio.

1958-59
Received Fulbright Fellowship; painted in Florence and Rome, Italy.

1960
Returned to New York.

1961
Received Louis Comfort Tiffany Foundation Fellowship.

1966
Taught at University of California, Davis, October to December; met William Allan and William Wiley.

1967-69
Returned to New York; taught at The School of Visual Arts, New York.

1968
Began single image paintings. Married Judy Davis; sons Robert and Matthew. Moved to Bennington, Vermont.

1969
Settled permanently in California; taught summer session at University of California, Berkeley. Daughter Rachel born.

1969-73
Taught at Sacramento State College, California.

1972
Painted *Landscape*. Established relationship with Nancy Hoffman Gallery, New York. Began *Water Painting* series. Son Reuben born.

1973
Began taking own photographs for paintings; painted *Muir Creek I*. Travelled to Scotland; began *Black Craig* series. Stopped teaching.

1974
Received first prize, Tokyo International Biennale, Japan.

1975
Travelled to Hawaii for the United States Department of the Interior exhibition, *America 1976*; began *Water Lily* series. Received first prize and purchase award, *Prints California* exhibition held at The Oakland Museum, California.

1977
Travelled to the Orient.

Biography

One-Man Exhibitions

1958
Kanegis Gallery, Boston, Massachusetts
November 1-27

1959
Galleria Numero, Florence, Italy

1963
d'Arcy Gallery, New York
Two exhibitions: February 18-March 9;
?-November 16

1965
Stable Gallery, New York
September 28-October 16

1966
Stable Gallery, New York
October 11-29

1967
Galleria Sperone, Turin, Italy
March-April

1968
Berkeley Gallery, San Francisco
May 28-June 22

Stable Gallery, New York
December 14, 1968-January 9, 1969

1969
Worth Ryder Gallery, University of
California, Berkeley
August 8-31

ASSSC Art Gallery, Sacramento State
College, California
October 23-November 21

1970
The Wichita Art Museum, Kansas
January

Reese Palley, San Francisco
September 10-October 17
Catalog published

1971
Art Gallery, University of California,
San Diego
November 16-December 10

1972
Reese Palley Gallery, New York
February 5-26

Nancy Hoffman Gallery, New York
December 9, 1972-January 4, 1973

1973
Joseph Raffael: Water Paintings
University Art Museum, Berkeley, California
July 18-September 16
Catalog published; also shown at Nancy
Hoffman Gallery, New York, October 13-
November 7, 1973; Museum of Contem-
porary Art, Chicago, March 9-April 28, 1974

1974
Nancy Hoffman Gallery, New York
November 2-28

Barbara Okun Gallery, St. Louis, Missouri
November

1975
UNLV Art Gallery, University of Nevada,
Las Vegas
October 26-November 7

Norman MacKenzie Art Gallery, University
of Regina, Saskatchewan, Canada
December 5, 1975-January 18, 1976
Catalog published

1976
Braunstein/Quay Gallery and Quay
Ceramics Gallery, San Francisco
March 30-April 24

Nancy Hoffman Gallery, New York
October 2-November 4

1977
Arco Center for Visual Art, Los Angeles
March 1-April 9

Raffael (with Judy Raffael)
Roy Boyd Gallery, Chicago
March 11-May 5

Museum of Fine Arts, St. Petersburg,
Florida
November 23, 1977-January 8, 1978

Selected Group Exhibitions

1965
*The Society for Contemporary American
Art 25th Annual Exhibition*, The Art Institute
of Chicago.

1966
Art in the Mirror, The Museum of Modern
Art, New York. Brochure published;
circulating exhibition.

Art on Paper 1966, Weatherspoon Art
Gallery, University of North Carolina at
Greensboro. Catalog published.

Highlights of the 1965-66 Art Season, The
Larry Aldrich Museum, Ridgefield,
Connecticut. Catalog published.

The Other Tradition, Institute of
Contemporary Art, University of
Pennsylvania, Philadelphia. Catalog
published.

The Photographic Image, The Solomon R.
Guggenheim Museum, New York. Catalog
published.

*The Society for Contemporary American
Art 26th Annual Exhibition*, The Art Institute
of Chicago.

1967
Annual Acquisitions Exhibition, Student
Union, University of Massachusetts,
Amherst. Catalog published.

*Art in Process: Visual Development of a
Collage*, Finch College Museum of Art, New
York. Catalog published.

*Contemporary American Painting and
Sculpture 1967*, Krannert Art Museum,
University of Illinois, Champaign. Catalog
published.

1st Kent International, Art Gallery, Kent
State University, Ohio.

Five Artists Show Collage, Gertrude Kasle Gallery, Detroit, Michigan.

Protest and Hope, Wollman Hall, New School Art Center, New York. Catalog published.

Salone Internazionale dei Giovanni, Galleria d'Arte Moderna, Milan, Italy.

Social Comment in America, The Museum of Modern Art, New York. Circulating exhibition.

30th Biennial Exhibition of Contemporary American Painting, The Corcoran Gallery of Art, Washington, D.C. Catalog published.

1968
Contemporary Drawings: Pop, Op and Other Recent Trends, The American Federation of Arts, New York. Circulating exhibition.

Magic and Super-Realism, Lowe Art Museum, University of Miami, Coral Gables, Florida.

The New Vein, International Art Program, National Collection of Fine Arts, Smithsonian Institution, Washington, D.C. Catalogs published by each exhibiting institution; exhibition shown in Belgrade, Yugoslavia; Cologne, Germany; Baden-Baden, Germany; Geneva, Switzerland; Brussels, Belgium; Milan, Italy.

The Obsessive Image 1960-1968, Institute of Contemporary Arts, London. Catalog published.

Patriotic Images in American Art, The American Federation of Arts, New York. Circulating exhibition.

São Paulo 9: United States of America (United States section at *IX Bienal*, Museu de Arte Moderna, São Paulo, Brazil), organized by National Collection of Fine Arts, Smithsonian Institution, Washington, D.C. Catalog published.

Selections from Hanford Yang Collection, The Larry Aldrich Museum, Ridgefield, Connecticut.

Violence in Recent American Art, Museum of Contemporary Art, Chicago. Catalog published.

1969
American Painting: The 1960's, The American Federation of Arts, New York. Catalog published; circulating exhibition.

The American Sense of Reality, Philbrook Art Center, Tulsa, Oklahoma. Catalog published; also shown at Museum of Art, University of Oklahoma, Norman, and Oklahoma Art Center, Oklahoma City.

Fulbright Artists, Smithsonian Institution, Washington, D.C. Circulating exhibition.

Human Concern/Personal Torment: The Grotesque in American Art, Whitney Museum of American Art, New York. Catalog published; also shown at University Art Museum, Berkeley, California.

Painting and Sculpture Today 1969, Indianapolis Museum of Art, Indiana. Catalog published.

Paintings from the Photo, The Riverside Museum, New York. Catalog published.

Repair Show, Berkeley Gallery, San Francisco. Also shown at ASSSC Art Gallery, Sacramento State College, California.

1970
American Painting 1970, Virginia Museum, Richmond. Catalog published.

Darmstadt Biennial, Darmstadt, Germany.

Directly Seen: New Realism in California, Newport Harbor Art Museum, Balboa, California. Catalog published.

Excellence: Art from the University Community, University Art Museum, Berkeley, California. Catalog published.

Looking West 1970, Joslyn Art Museum, Omaha, Nebraska. Catalog published.

1971
Contemporary American Art from Orange County Collections, Newport Harbor Art Museum, Newport Beach, California. Catalog published.

A Decade in the West: Painting, Sculpture and Graphics from the Anderson Collection, Stanford University Museum of Art, Stanford, California. Catalog published; also shown at Santa Barbara Museum of Art, California.

The 73rd Western Annual, Denver Art Museum, Colorado. Catalog published.

1972
Phases of New Realism, Lowe Art Museum, University of Miami, Coral Gables, Florida. Catalog published.

Realism Now, New York Cultural Center, New York. Catalog published.

Sacramento Sampler I, E.B. Crocker Art Gallery, Sacramento, California. Catalog published; also shown at The Oakland Museum, California.

Seventieth American Exhibition, The Art Institute of Chicago. Catalog published.

1973
The Emerging Real, Storm King Art Center, Mountainville, New York.

New Acquisitions for the Now and Future Museum, Long Beach Museum of Art, California. Catalog published.

1973 Biennial Exhibition: Contemporary American Art, Whitney Museum of American Art, New York. Catalog published.

Options 73/30, Contemporary Arts Center, Cincinnati, Ohio. Catalog published.

Separate Realities, Los Angeles Municipal Art Gallery. Catalog published.

SoHo in Potsdam, Brainerd Hall Art Gallery, State University College at Potsdam, New York.

The Super Realist Vision, DeCordova Museum, Lincoln, Massachusetts. Catalog published.

1974
Art in Embassies program, United States State Department, Washington, D.C.

Collector's Choice, Elvehjem Art Center, University of Wisconsin-Madison.

Contemporary American Painting and Sculpture 1974, Krannert Art Museum, University of Illinois, Urbana-Champaign. Catalog published.

Drawings, Nancy Hoffman Gallery, New York. Catalog published; also shown at Lowe Art Museum, University of Miami, Coral Gables, Florida.

New Editions, Montgomery Art Center, Pomona College, Claremont, California.

New Images in Painting, Tokyo International Biennale, Japan. Catalog published.

New/Photo Realism, Wadsworth Atheneum, Hartford, Connecticut. Catalog published.

New Realism Revisited, Brainerd Hall Art Gallery, State University College at Potsdam, New York. Catalog published.

New York Avant-Garde, Saidye Bronfman Centre of the YM-YWHA, Montreal, Canada. Catalog published.

1974 Art on Paper, Weatherspoon Art Gallery, University of North Carolina at Greensboro. Catalog published.

Painting and Sculpture Today 1974, Indianapolis Museum of Art, Indiana. Catalog published; also shown at The Contemporary Art Center and Taft Museum, Cincinnati, Ohio.

Seventy-first American Exhibition, The Art Institute of Chicago. Catalog published.

Three Realists: Close, Estes, Raffael, Worcester Art Museum, Massachusetts. Catalog published.

1975
Contemporary Landscape Painting, Oklahoma Art Center, Oklahoma City. Catalog published.

Prints California, The Oakland Museum, California. Catalog published; also shown at Santa Barbara Museum of Art, California.

A Response to the Environment, Rutgers University Art Gallery, New Brunswick, New Jersey. Catalog published.

Watercolors and Drawings—American Realists, Louis K. Meisel Gallery, New York. Catalog published.

1976
America 1976, United States Department of the Interior, Washington, D.C. Catalog published; exhibition shown at Corcoran Gallery of Art, Washington, D.C.; Wadsworth Atheneum, Hartford, Connecticut; Fogg Art Museum, Cambridge, Massachusetts, and Institute of Contemporary Art, Boston; Minneapolis Institute of Arts, Minnesota; Milwaukee Art Center, Wisconsin; The Fort Worth Art Museum, Texas; San Francisco Museum of Modern Art; The High Museum of Art, Atlanta, Georgia; The Brooklyn Museum, New York.

America 1976: Source Material and Related Works, Boston University Art Gallery, Massachusetts.

Art as Likeness, Art Gallery, Moravian College, Bethlehem, Pennsylvania. Catalog published.

Aspects of Realism from the Nancy Hoffman Gallery, Art Gallery, O'Shaughnessy Hall, University of Notre Dame, Indiana. Catalog published.

Collector's Choice, Philbrook Art Center, Tulsa, Oklahoma.

Contemporary Images in Watercolor, Akron Art Institute, Ohio. Catalog published; also shown at Indianapolis Museum of Art, Indiana; Memorial Art Gallery, University of Rochester, New York.

Endangered Species: The Artist or the Cow?, Point Reyes Gallery of Fine Art, Point Reyes Station, California.

Florists' Transworld Delivery Collection, Michael C. Rockefeller Arts Center Gallery, New York. Catalog published.

The Hue and Far Cry of Color, Fort Wayne Museum of Art, Indiana.

Painting and Sculpture in California: The Modern Era, San Francisco Museum of Modern Art. Catalog published; also shown at National Collection of Fine Arts, Smithsonian Institution, Washington, D.C.

Painting and Sculpture Today 1976, Indianapolis Museum of Art, Indiana. Catalog published.

Possibilities for Collectors, Des Moines Art Center, Iowa.

Seventy-second American Exhibition, The Art Institute of Chicago. Catalog published.

Watercolor U.S.A.: National Invitational Exhibition, Springfield Art Museum, Missouri. Catalog published.

1977
American Painterly Realism, Heath Gallery, Atlanta, Georgia. Also shown at Simone Stern Gallery, New Orleans.

California Viewpoints, Roy Boyd Gallery, Chicago.

Drawings of the 70's, Society for Contemporary Art, The Art Institute of Chicago. Brochure published.

8 Contemporary American Realists, Pennsylvania Academy of the Fine Arts, Philadelphia. Catalog published; also shown at North Carolina Museum of Art, Raleigh.

Group Show, Barbara Okun Gallery, Creve Coeur, Missouri.

Illusion and Reality, Australia Council, North Sydney. Catalog published; exhibition shown at Australian National Gallery, Canberra; Western Australian Art Gallery, Perth; Queensland Art Gallery, Brisbane; Art Gallery of New South Wales, Sydney; Art Gallery of South Australia, Adelaide; National Gallery of Victoria, Melbourne; Tasmanian Museum and Art Gallery, Hobart.

New Realism, Jacksonville Art Museum, Florida. Catalog published.

Perceptions of the Spirit in Twentieth-Century American Art, Indianapolis Museum of Art, Indiana. Catalog published; also shown at University Art Museum, Berkeley, California; Marion Koogler McNay Art Institute, San Antonio, Texas; Columbus Gallery of Fine Arts, Ohio.

Private Images: Photographs by Painters, Los Angeles County Museum of Art. Brochure published.

Realist Prints, Australia Council, North Sydney. Exhibition shown at Australian National Gallery, Canberra; Western Australian Art Gallery, Perth; Queensland Art Gallery, Brisbane; Art Gallery of New South Wales, Sydney; Art Gallery of South Australia, Adelaide; National Gallery of Victoria, Melbourne; Tasmanian Museum and Art Gallery, Hobart.

Representations of America, The Metropolitan Museum of Art, New York. Exhibition shown at Hermitage Museum, Leningrad; Alexander Pushkin Museum of Fine Arts, Moscow; State Gallery of Byelorussia, Minsk.

30 Years of American Art, 1945-1975: Selections from the Permanent Collection, Whitney Museum of American Art, New York.

A View of a Decade, Museum of Contemporary Art, Chicago. Catalog published.

Watercolors and Related Media by Contemporary Californians, Baxter Art Gallery, California Institute of Technology, Pasadena. Catalog published.

West Coast Art 1970-76, Gallery 210, University of Missouri, St. Louis.

Wish I Were There, Fendrick Gallery, Washington, D.C.

Selected Bibliography

Books

Battcock, Gregory. *Super Realism: A Critical Anthology.* New York: E. P. Dutton & Co., Inc., 1975, pp. 49, 51, 56, 58-59, 212-222 (ill.).

Schinneller, James A. *Art/Search and Self-Discovery.* Third edition. Worcester, Massachusetts: Davis Publications, Inc., 1975, p. 119 (ill.).

Articles

A.A. "Joseph Raffael." *The Village Voice,* October 7-13, 1976.

Adlow, Dorothy. "Raffaele at Kanegis." *The Christian Science Monitor*, November 7, 1958.

Albright, Thomas. "At the Galleries." *San Francisco Chronicle*, April 3, 1976, p. 34.

_____. "Bumper Crop." *The Art Gallery*, Vol. XIV, No. 3, December 1970, p. 9 (ill.).

_____. "Jazzing Up the Corporate Image." *San Francisco Chronicle*, March 11, 1972, p. 33 (ill.).

_____. "Print Competition Display at Oakland." *This World, San Francisco Sunday Chronicle and Examiner*, May 11, 1975, p. 29 (ill.).

_____. "San Francisco: Thinking Small: Chamber works and futuristic visions." *Art News*, Vol. 75, No. 6, Summer 1976, p. 146.

_____. "A Triple-Threat Artist." *San Francisco Chronicle*, September 15, 1970, p. 38 (ill.).

Allman, Paul. "Art Who? finds new talents." *Richmond Independent* [California], September 1, 1973.

Alloway, Lawrence. "Art." *The Nation*, Vol. 209, No. 23, December 29, 1969, pp. 741-742.

_____. "Art as Likeness: with a note on Post Pop Art." *Arts Magazine*, Vol. 41, No. 7, May 1967, pp. 34-39 (ill.).

L.A. (Laurie Anderson). "Reviews and Previews." *Art News*, Vol. 71, No. 1, March 1972, pp. 21, 53.

"Art &." *The Village Voice*, December 21, 1972.

"Art in New York." *Time*, Vol. 88, No. 18, October 28, 1966, p. NY1.

"Art in New York." *Time*, Vol. 93, No. 1, January 3, 1969, p. NY1.

Artner, Alan G. "An Imagist's Showing While the Battles Go On." *Chicago Tribune*, March 24, 1974 (ill.).

Ashton, Dore. "An evolution illuminated." *Studio International*, Vol. 171, No. 875, March 1966, p. 114 (ill.).

M.B. "Joseph Raffael Paintings." *Artists Review Art*, Vol. 2, No. 2, October 1976.

J.B. (Jacqueline Barnitz). "In the Galleries." *Arts Magazine*, Vol. 40, No. 2, December 1965, p. 60.

Benedikt, Michael. "New York Letter." *Art International*, Vol. IX, No. 8, November 20, 1965, pp. 44-45, 50 (ill.).

Berkman, Florence. "Three Realists: A Cold, Plastic World." *The Hartford Times* [Connecticut], March 10, 1974, pp. 51-53.

Bruner, Louise. "Directions in Painting: Comments on 3 Shows." *The Blade* [Toledo, Ohio], October 22, 1967.

Burke, Lora. "Calif. Artist Featured at Norman Mackenzie." *The Leader Post* [Regina, Canada], December 20, 1975, p. 6.

Butler, Joseph T. "America." *The Connoisseur*, Vol. 186, No. 748, June 1974, pp. 142-143 (ill.).

_____. "The American Way with Art." *The Connoisseur*, Vol. 175, No. 700, June 1970, pp. 162-163 (ill.).

Butterfield, Jan. " 'I Have Always Copied': an Interview with Joseph Raffael." *Arts Magazine*, Vol. 51, No. 2, October 1976, pp. 122-126 (ill.).

Canaday, John. "Art: Surprising Show by Miss Bieser." *The New York Times*, December 23, 1972.

Carver, Mabel MacDonald. "Raffaele: Clear Dealer in Color." *The Villager* [New York], November 14, 1963 (ill.).

Cervenak, Tom. "Guests, spillover and weekenders." *Pacific Sun* [Mill Valley, California], August 20-26, 1976.

Chandler, John Noel. "Notes toward a new aesthetic." *Artscanada*, Nos. 172/173, October/November 1972, pp. 16-25 (ill.).

Clay, Kinky. *The Washington Post*, January 29, 1977, p. E7 (ill.).

Coke, Van Deren. "Albuquerque: Crucial Grants." *Art News*, Vol. 74, No. 2, February 1975, pp. 67-68.

Cornell, Peter and Staffan Cullberg. "New York, September-Oktober, 1967." *Konstrevy* [Stockholm, Sweden], No. 1, 1968, pp. 12-16 (ill.).

Deschin, Jacob. "Photography." *The New York Times*, January 4, 1970.

Dunham, Judith L. "Joseph Raffael Paintings: In and Under Water." *Artweek* [Oakland, California], Vol. 7, No. 16, April 17, 1976, pp. 1, 16 (ill.).

Fitz Gibbon, John. "Sacramento!" *Art in America*, Vol. 59, No. 6, November-December 1971, pp. 78-83 (ill.).

French, Palmer D. "San Francisco." *Artforum*, Vol. VII, No. 3, November 1968, p. 65 (ill.).

Fuller, Mary. "The Water Becomes the Lily, An Interview with Joseph Raffael." *Currânt* [San Francisco], Vol. 2, No. 2, August-September-October 1976, pp. 16-22 (ill.).

Gilbert-Rolfe, Jeremy. "Reviews." *Artforum*, Vol. XII, No. 5, January 1974, pp. 71-72 (ill.).

Glueck, Grace. "Oh, To Be Born Under Pisces, With Sagittarius Rising." *The New York Times*, December 29, 1968, pp. 25, 27 (ill.).

Greenwood, Michael. "Current Representational Art: Five Other Visions: Duane Hanson & Joseph Raffael." *Artscanada*, Vol. XXXIII, No. 4, December 1976/January 1977, pp. 23-29 (ill.).

Gruen, John. "Eight Soho Shows." *The Soho Weekly News* [New York], November 14, 1974, p. 18 (ill.).

____. "The Extended Vision." *New York Magazine*, Vol. 3, No. 2, January 12, 1970.

____. "What Painters See in Photographs." *New York World Journal Tribune*, October 23, 1966, pp. 35-36.

Haydon, Harold. "Contrasting Styles in Flock of Current Shows." *Showcase, Chicago Sun-Times*, March 17, 1974, p. 14.

Henry, Gerrit. "Reviews." *Art News*, Vol. 75, No. 10, December 1976, p. 122.

Hughes, Robert. "Face of the Land." *Time*, Vol. 108, No. 1, July 5, 1976, pp. 78-80.

____. "The Last Salon." *Time*, Vol. 101, No. 7, February 12, 1973, p. 46 (ill.).

____. "A Slice of the River." *Time*, Vol. 102, No. 16, October 15, 1973, pp. 112-113 (ill.).

Johnson, Charles. "Art Reviews." *The Sacramento Bee* [California], September 27, 1970, p. L15 (ill.).

____. "Artists Are Returning to Realism, But Not Realism of Photography." *The Sacramento Bee* [California], November 2, 1969, pp. L14-L15 (ill.).

____. " 'New Realism' Can Be A Distant, Floating Fish." *The Sacramento Bee* [California], July 22, 1973 (ill.).

D.J. (Donald Judd). "In the Galleries." *Arts Magazine*, Vol. 37, No. 7, April 1963, p. 61.

Kelley, Mary Lou. "Pop-Art inspired objective realism." *The Christian Science Monitor*, April 1, 1974.

Kingsley, April. "New York Letter." *Art International*, Vol. XVII, No. 3, March 1973, pp. 49-50 (ill.).

Kuspit, Donald B. "Review of Exhibitions." *Art in America*, Vol. 65, No. 2, March-April 1977, pp. 115-116.

"Landscape on the Horizon." *The Village Voice*, December 2, 1974.

Lichtblau, Charlotte. "Painters Use of Photographs Explored." *The Philadelphia Inquirer*, February 1, 1970.

L. L. (Lillian Lonngren). "Reviews and Previews." *Art News*, Vol. 62, No. 7, November 1963, p. 48.

Lubell, Ellen. "Art Reviews." *Arts Magazine*, Vol. 49, No. 5, January 1975, p. 9.

____. "Galleries." *Arts Magazine*, Vol. 47, No. 4, February 1973, pp. 81-82 (ill.).

____. "Joseph Raffael." *Arts Magazine*, Vol. 51, No. 4, December 1976, p. 34 (ill.).

____. "New York Galleries." *Arts Magazine*, Vol. 48, No. 3, December 1973, p. 63 (ill.).

Markell, Jon. "Joseph Raffael and Los Angeles Artists." *Daily Californian* [University of California, Berkeley], August 9, 1973 (ill.).

McCann, Cecile N. "Joseph Raffael 'Water Paintings.' " *Artweek* [Oakland, California], Vol. 4, No. 28, September 1, 1973, pp. 1, 12 (ill.).

____. "Joyous Art." *Artweek* [Oakland, California], Vol. 1, No. 31, September 19, 1970, p. 1 (ill.).

Mellow, James R. "New York Letter." *Art International*, Vol. X, No. 10, December 20, 1966, pp. 62-63 (ill.).

"The Modest British Push Ahead." *The Economist*, April 7, 1973.

Muchnic, Suzanne. "First View of a Corporate Collection." *Artweek* [Oakland, California], Vol. 8, No. 2, January 8, 1977, p. 5.

Muldavin, Albie and John Noel Chandler. "Correspondences." *Artscanada*, Nos. 156/157, June/July 1971, pp. 44-49 (ill.).

Nemser, Cindy. "The Closeup Vision—Representational Art—Part II." *Arts Magazine*, Vol. 46, No. 7, May 1972, pp. 44-48.

C.N. (Cindy Nemser). "In the Museums." *Arts Magazine*, Vol. 44, No. 3, December 1969-January 1970, p. 56.

"New Talent USA: Joe Raffaele." *Art in America*, Vol. 54, No. 4, July-August 1966, p. 34 (ill.).

"Painting: Unphotography." *Time*, Vol. 93, No. 15, April 11, 1969, pp. 80-81 (ill.).

Perreault, John. "Art." *The Village Voice*, February 17, 1972.

____. "Art: Get the Picture?" *The Village Voice*, December 18, 1969, pp. 18, 46.

____. "Get Back." *The Village Voice*, February 1970, pp. 14-18.

____. "Postcards and a plastic rose." *The Village Voice*, October 25, 1973, p. 41.

____. "Tokyo: Paris of tomorrow?" *The Village Voice*, September 19, 1974, pp. 46-48.

V. P. (Valerie Petersen). "Reviews and Previews." *Art News*, Vol. 62, No. 1, March 1963, p. 17.

Picard, Lil. "Art." *The East Village Other* [New York], October 1966.

Pincus-Witten, Robert. "Allusive Structure: A Conversation with Joe Raffaele." *Artforum*, Vol. V, No. 4, December 1966, pp. 20-21 (ill.).

____. "Joe Raffaele, Stable Gallery." *Artforum*, Vol. IV, No. 4, December 1965, p. 51 (ill.).

____. "New York: The Photographic Image, Guggenheim Museum." *Artforum*, Vol. IV, No. 7, March 1966, p. 47.

The Print Collector's Newsletter, Vol. VII, No. 3, July-August 1976, p. 88.

The Print Collector's Newsletter, Vol. VII, No. 6, January-February 1977, p. 182.

"Raffael Art Shown Here." *Las Vegas Review Journal* [Nevada], October 19, 1975, p. 2B.

Raffaele, Joe. "Letters" (letter to editor). *The East Village Other* [New York], April 15-May 1, 1967, p. 2.

Raffaele, Joe and Elizabeth Baker. "The Way-Out West: Interviews with 4 San Francisco Artists." *Art News*, Vol. 66, No. 4, Summer 1967, pp. 38-41, 72-76.

Raffaele, Joe and Peter Saul. "Los Angeles: Subversive Art." *Arts Magazine*, Vol. 41, No. 7, May 1967, pp. 50-52.

Ratcliff, Carter. "New York." *Art International*, Vol. XIV, No. 3, March 20, 1970, pp. 67-68 (ill.).

_____. "New York Letter." *Art International*, Vol. XVI, No. 4, April 20, 1972, pp. 34-35 (ill.).

"Realist Painting exhibition to open on Wednesday." *Evening News* [Southbridge, Massachusetts], February 25, 1974.

Richardson, Brenda. "Bay Area Survey." *Arts Magazine*, Vol. 45, No. 2, November 1970, p. 54 (ill.).

Rose, Barbara. "New York Letter." *Art International*, Vol. VII, No. 9, December 5, 1963, p. 65 (ill.).

Rosenthal, Adrienne. "Joseph Raffael—Studies in Metamorphosis." *Artweek* [Oakland, California], Vol. 8, No. 13, March 26, 1977, p. 3 (ill.).

Rubinfein, Leo. "Reviews New York." *Artforum*, Vol. XV, No. 4, December 1976, p. 66 (ill.).

Russell, John. "Art: Beyond Good and Bad Taste." *The New York Times*, October 8, 1976.

_____. "Reviews." *The New York Times*, November 16, 1974.

G.S. "Coronata da grande successo la nuova mostra di Raffaele." *Il Progresso Italo-Americano*, November 13, 1963, p. 9 (ill.).

L.H.S. (Lynn H. Schafran). "Reviews and Previews." *Art News*, Vol. 67, No. 10, February 1969, pp. 20, 22 (ill.).

Selz, Peter. "Six artists in search of a definition of San Francisco." *Art News*, Vol. 72, No. 6, Summer 1973, pp. 34-37 (ill.).

Shere, Charles. "U.C. Shows New Raffael Paintings." *Oakland Tribune* [California], July 27, 1973.

"Shows Illinois." *Midwest Art*, March 1974, p. 14 (ill.).

Siegel, Jeanne. "Reviews and Previews." *Art News*, Vol. 72, No. 10, December 1973, p. 97.

Smith, Corinna. "Fall Comes to Soho." *The Soho Weekly News* [New York], October 14, 1976, p. 23.

Spear, Marilyn W. "Three Realists Showing At Museum." *Worcester Telegram* [Massachusetts], February 27, 1974.

Stevens, Carol. "Message into Medium: Photography as an Artist's Tool." *Print*, Vol. 24, No. 3, May-June 1970, p. 57 (ill.).

Stevens, Elizabeth. "The Camera's Eye on Canvas." *The Wall Street Journal*, January 6, 1970, p. 16.

Swain, Richard. "In the Galleries." *Arts Magazine*, Vol. 40, No. 5, March 1966, p. 52.

Swenson, G.R. "Paint, Flesh, Vesuvius." *Arts Magazine*, Vol. 41, No. 1, November 1966, pp. 33-35 (ill.).

G.R.S. (G.R. Swenson). "Reviews and Previews." *Art News*, Vol. 64, No. 5, September 1965, p. 18.

Tager, Ruth. "Chicago Exhibit Features 3 Contemporary Artists." *The Courier* [Champaign-Urbana, Illinois], March 31, 1974.

Tarshis, Jerome. "San Francisco." *Artforum*, Vol. IX, No. 4, December 1970, pp. 83-84 (ill.).

Taylor, Robert. "Raffaele Paintings." *The Boston Sunday Herald*, November 16, 1958.

F.T. (Frederic Tuten). "In the Galleries: Joseph Raffael." *Arts Magazine*, Vol. 43, No. 4, February 1969, p. 62 (ill.).

"Two Raffaels." *Chicago Daily News*, March 19-20, 1977.

Wahl, Kenneth. "Landscape Renaissance." *The Soho Weekly News* [New York], November 4, 1976, p. 20 (ill.).

D.W. (Diane Waldman). "Reviews and Previews." *Art News*, Vol. 65, No. 7, November 1966, pp. 64, 66.

Wasserman, Emily. "Joseph Raffael/Carlos Villa/Hank Gobin: To make the painting look at you . . ." *Artforum*, Vol. IX, No. 5, January 1971, pp. 54-57 (ill.).

Wasserman, Jeanne L. "An American Documentary." *Harvard Magazine*, Vol. 79, No. 5, January-February 1977, pp. 45-47 (ill.).

" 'Water Paintings' at UAM." *Vallejo Times-Herald* [California], July 29, 1973 (ill.).

Weeks, H.J. "Prints California." *Artweek* [Oakland, California], Vol. 6, No. 24, June 28, 1975, pp. 1, 20 (ill.).

Wilson, William. "The Paintings of Joe Raffaele: In the Franciscan Mood." *Art and Artists*, Vol. I, No. 6, September 1966, pp. 22-27 (ill.).

_____. "The Paintings of Joseph Raffael." *Studio International*, Vol. 187, No. 966, May 1974, pp. 242-244 (ill.).

_____. " 'Realities' Mirrors a Tragic Flaw." *Los Angeles Times*, September 30, 1973.

Wolmer, Denise. "In the Galleries." *Arts Magazine*, Vol. 46, No. 6, April 1972, p. 66.

"Worcester Art Museum hosts major painting exhibition." *Enterprise-Sun* [Marlboro, Massachusetts], February 26, 1974.

Wortz, Melinda. "Joseph Raffael at Arco Center." *Los Angeles Times,* March 16, 1977, p. IV: 8.

_____. "New Editions." *Artweek* [Oakland, California], Vol. 5, No. 35, October 19, 1974, pp. 1, 16 (ill.).

Zickerman, Lynne. "In Art with Joseph Raffael." *The Daily Californian* [University of California, Berkeley], October 20, 1972, pp. 12-13 (ill.).

Zucker, Barbara. "New York Reviews." *Art News*, Vol. 74, No. 2, February 1975, p. 97.

Films
Smith, Gloria (author, producer, director). *The eyes have it: Joseph Raffael.* Film shown in Sacramento, California: KCRA (NBC-TV), 1972.

Photography Credits

Cover photograph by Joseph Raffael.

On pages 2, 3, 7, 8 and 10, color photographs by Dennis Gray, black and white photographs by Dennis Gray/Thomas H. Garver.

Except in those cases listed below, all photographs of works of art reproduced were taken by Schopplein Studio and have been supplied by the artist. The numbers listed refer to checklist numbers.

E.B. Crocker Art Gallery, Sacramento, California, 7
The Fine Arts Museums of San Francisco:
M.H. de Young Memorial Museum, 20
Walter and Nancy Griffith, Omaha, Nebraska, 3
John Berggruen Gallery, San Francisco, 36
Joslyn Art Museum, Omaha, Nebraska, 1
Nancy Hoffman Gallery, New York, 5, 8, 11, 15, 26

Design: Ross
Printing: Phelps/Schaefer
Litho-Graphics
Type composed in Helvetica
on the Merganthaler V-I-P
by Custom Typography Service